Guests Without Stress

Guests Without Stress

Elizabeth Hill • Martha Starr • Ann Upton

EPM Publications
McLean, Virginia

Library of Congress Cataloging-in-Publication Data

Hill, Elizabeth.
Guests without stress : a cookbook : great recipes and menus to make ahead / Elizabeth Hill, Martha Starr, Ann Upton.
p. cm.
Includes index.
ISBN 1-889324-01-9
1. Make-ahead cookery. 2. Entertaining. 3. Menus. I. Starr, Martha. II. Upton, Ann. III. Title.
TX652.H544 1997
641.5'55—dc20 96-35993
CIP

EPM Publications, Inc., 1003 Turkey Run Road
McLean, Virginia 22101

Printed in the United States of America

Book design by Martha Starr
Cover design by Nan Starr

Dedicated to all cooks who enjoy the warmth of sharing a meal with friends, the feeling of time standing still while they participate in one of the oldest rituals in the human experience.

Things haven't changed that much

Contents

You might even have time for this . . .

Introduction

Guests Without Stress is our response to something we have all experienced—stress when having guests for dinner. This book will help you to plan and prepare a good dinner in a way that allows you to be more relaxed when the doorbell rings and to get out of the kitchen to enjoy your guests.

Much last-minute frenzy can be avoided by preparing, combining and cooking most of the meal well ahead of time. A sauce can be made, celery chopped, cheese grated, and peppers roasted two or three days ahead, leaving the fewest possible tasks to the last minute.

We have carefully chosen recipes with this in mind. Directions are written as "Countdowns" to indicate just how far ahead you can do each step. Our timing allows thirty minutes for gathering over drinks and about ten minutes to enjoy the first course before you serve the entrée. Adjust this timing to suit your own schedule.

Our Suggested Menus combine first courses, entrées and desserts which work well together for taste and texture, and which avoid conflicts in last minute activities and oven temperatures.

Relax! These recipes are forgiving, and easy on the cook. The ingredients are readily available in the markets. There are no soufflés to make you or your guests nervous. We even provide a safety net—see Cook's Special Dessert on page 114.

We are confident that you are going to have a great time with this book. We have.

Go for it—*ahead* of time!

– Liz Hill, Marty Starr and Ann Upton

Suggested Menus

One cannot think well, love well, sleep well,
if one has not dined well. –Virginia Woolf

Danish Blue Cheese Mousse
Beef with Almonds & Apricots
Wine Red Jelly

Mushrooms on Spinach with Shaved Parmesan
Lamb in a Packet with Skordalia Sauce
Apples Grand Marnier

Carrot & Orange Soup
Ham Loaf with Spinach-Pear Purée
Flawless Flourless Chocolate Cake

Sliced Cucumbers with Orange-Grapefruit Dressing
Casablanca Chicken
No Peel, No Chop, No Cook Delicious Dessert

Tango Soup
Salmon Fillets with Leeks, Carrots & Mushrooms
Pineapple Victoria with Strawberries

Shrimp Salad with Olives, Celery & Snow Peas
Eggplant Lasagna
Lemon Chess Pie

Celery Root & Beets with Apple Vinaigrette
Beef with a Southern Accent
Savannah Orange Pie

Green Beans with Pecan Sauce
Lamb Chops with Feta Cheese & Rosemary Potatoes
Chocolate Brandy Pudding Cake

Herbed Tomato Soup
Pork Tenderloins, Chutney Cream & Artichoke-Lima Bean Salad
Fantastic Fruit Compote

Artichoke Hearts with Roasted Pepper Sauce
Ginger Cream Chicken with Bulghur Pilaf
Oranges Araby

Leek & Red Pepper Salad
Lemon-Dill Fish with Sweet Potato Slices
Little Ginger Butter Cake with Mango Sorbet

Pesto Consommé with Walnuts
Vegetable Medley with Coconut Curry Sauce
Biscotti Ice Cream

Gazpacho
Steak Salad with Roquefort Dressing
Bronzy Bananas & Apricots

Salmon Mounds on Mixed Greens
Braised Lamb Shanks with White Beans
Pears in Red Wine

Apple Mint Soup
Barbecued-Indoors Country Ribs with Potato-Bean Salad
Strawberry Islands

Eggplant Rollups with Herbed Cheese
Glazed Cornish Hens with Rice Verde
Pristine Pears

Mushroom Bisque
Trout on Wild Rice with Carrots Vinaigrette
Rum Chocolate Mousse

Scallops on a Bed of Celery
Cheese Strata with Baked Spinach Tomatoes
Fruit Fondue

Asparagus with Nutty Vinaigrette
Veal Estouffade with Potato Gratin
Mocha Crème Brulée

Goat Cheese & Sun-Dried Tomatoes on Red-Leaf Lettuce
Lamb Bombay
Gingered Ice Cream with Strawberry-Rhubarb Sauce

Squash Bisque
Chicken Breasts & Artichoke Purée with Romaine Couscous
Macaroon Pie

Prosciutto & Cashew Nut Salad
Flounder on Ratatouille
Peaches Cointreau

Mushrooms & Roasted Red Peppers
Spicy Macaroni with Mulled Grapes
Strawberry Tart

Soups

Cooking is like love. It should be entered into with abandon or not at all.

– Harriet Van Horne

Apple Mint Soup

Serves 6

A subtle combination of flavors that will keep your guests guessing

YOU WILL NEED

2 tablespoons butter
1 medium yellow onion
1 teaspoon mild curry powder
4 cups chicken broth
4 medium cooking apples
2 tablespoons mango chutney
Juice of half a lemon
8 sprigs fresh mint
Salt and freshly ground pepper
½ cup plain yogurt

THE COUNTDOWN

Two days ahead:

1. Melt the butter in a large skillet. Coarsely chop the onion, add it to the skillet and cook gently until soft. Add the curry powder and stir constantly for one or two minutes. Add the chicken broth.
2. Peel, core and coarsely chop the apples. Add them to the skillet and bring to a boil, stirring. Reduce the heat, cover and simmer until the apples are tender, about 15 minutes.
3. Put the apple mixture into a food processor or blender. Add the chutney and lemon juice and blend until smooth.
4. Pull the leaves from all but one of the mint sprigs and chop fine.
5. Pour the soup into a large bowl and add the chopped mint, salt and pepper to taste. Cool, cover and refrigerate.

Thirty minutes before your guests are expected:

1. Whisk in the yogurt and adjust the seasonings. Thin with milk if desired.
2. Ladle into soup cups and garnish with mint leaves.

Carrot & Orange Soup

Serves 6

Don't let the simple ingredients fool you. Very tasty

YOU WILL NEED

- 2 tablespoons butter
- 1 tablespoon olive oil
- 1 onion, coarsely chopped
- 3 leeks, thinly sliced, white part only
- 1 pound carrots
- 3 cups chicken broth
- 1¾ cups fresh orange juice
- 1½ teaspoons curry powder
- 1/8 teaspoon each ground cloves, cayenne and nutmeg
- 1 teaspoon thyme
- Salt and freshly ground pepper

THE COUNTDOWN

One to three days ahead:

1. In a medium-sized pot, melt the butter, add the oil and sauté the onion and leeks until tender.
2. Peel and grate one large carrot for garnish. Place in a plastic bag and refrigerate.
3. Peel and chop the remaining carrots. Add the carrots and the chicken broth to the pot. Bring the mixture to a boil, reduce the heat and simmer until the carrots are tender.
4. Purée the vegetables with some of the broth and return to the pot.
5. Add the orange juice and seasonings. Cool and refrigerate.

At least an hour before your guests are expected:

1. Remove the pot of soup and the grated carrot from the refrigerator.

Fifteen minutes before:

1. Heat the soup slowly on the stove. Check the seasonings. When hot, turn the heat off and cover.

Just before serving:

1. Bring the soup to piping hot.
2. Put a teaspoon of grated carrot in each soup cup. Ladle in the soup and sprinkle with grated carrot.

Gazpacho

Serves 6

Like eating your way through a vegetable garden, crunch and yum

YOU WILL NEED

- 4 medium to large tomatoes
- 2 cucumbers
- 2 bunches scallions
- 1 green pepper
- 2 to 3 garlic cloves
- ¼ cup red wine vinegar
- ⅓ cup olive oil
- 3 small cans tomato juice
- Worcestershire and hot pepper sauce to taste
- Salt and freshly ground pepper
- 6 chilled soup bowls

THE COUNTDOWN

One or two days ahead:

1. Put the tomatoes in boiling water, turn off the heat, and let stand for 3 or 4 minutes. Remove with a slotted spoon, cool and peel.
2. Peel the cucumbers, discard the seeds and chop. Wash and chop the scallions. Core, seed and chop the green pepper.
3. Chop the tomatoes in a bowl, discarding the stems. Add the cucumbers, green pepper and scallions.

4. Mince the garlic and combine with the vinegar. Gradually whisk in the olive oil. Pour into the bowl with the tomatoes and stir. Add the tomato juice, Worcestershire sauce, hot pepper sauce, salt and pepper to taste. Cover and refrigerate.
5. Chill six soup bowls.

Just before serving:

1. Check the seasonings.
2. Spoon the soup into the chilled bowls and serve immediately.

Too good to share

Herbed Tomato Soup

Serves 6

So fresh tasting you'll feel like a fraud (the basic ingredient is from a can)

YOU WILL NEED

¼ cup salad oil

¼ cup vinegar

1 quart can plus 1 small can of tomato juice

¾ cup whole milk

2½ tablespoons lemon juice

2 garlic cloves, minced

2 tablespoons sugar

1 teaspoon dry mustard

3 tablespoons fresh rosemary leaves, or 1 tablespoon dried

3 tablespoons chopped fresh basil leaves, or 1 tablespoon dried

3 teaspoons fresh thyme leaves, or 1 teaspoon dried

Salt and freshly ground pepper

1 large cucumber

THE COUNTDOWN

Two or three days ahead:

1. Combine the oil, vinegar and tomato juice.
2. Beat in the milk and the lemon juice.
3. Add the garlic, sugar, mustard, herbs, salt and pepper. Chill.

One day ahead:

1. Peel and finely chop the cucumber. Place in a plastic bag and refrigerate.
2. Strain the soup, add salt and pepper and adjust seasonings. Cover and refrigerate.

Just before serving:

1. Take the soup and the cucumber from the refrigerator.
2. Place a spoonful of cucumber in each soup cup.
3. Pour in the soup.

Mushroom Bisque

Serves 6

Like a walk in deep woods …

YOU WILL NEED

2 pounds mixed fresh mushrooms: white, cremini, portobello, chanterelles and/or morels

4 or more tablespoons butter

8 shallots, peeled and chopped

4 or more cups chicken broth

¾ cup almonds

Salt and freshly ground pepper

½ cup heavy cream

1 cup chopped parsley for garnish

THE COUNTDOWN

Two or three days ahead:

1. Dampen a paper towel and wipe off any mushrooms that need cleaning. Coarsely chop and set aside.
2. In a large saucepan or Dutch oven, melt the butter, add the chopped shallots and sauté until soft.
3. Add the mushrooms, and more butter if necessary, and sauté until all the moisture from the mushrooms has evaporated.
4. Pour some of the broth into the saucepan and simmer for 8 to 10 minutes.
5. Add the almonds, pour the mixture into a food processor and purée. Return the purée to the saucepan, adding salt, pepper and more broth if needed. Add the heavy cream and check the seasonings. Refrigerate.

An hour before your guests are expected:

1. Take the soup from the refrigerator.

Thirty minutes before:

1. Reheat gently. Turn heat off and cover.

Just before serving:

1. Turn on the heat but do not boil.
2. Garnish with parsley.

Soup with a beard? It's an art

Pesto Consommé with Walnuts

Serves 6

A snap to make and always a hit

YOU WILL NEED

For the pesto, unless you buy it:

½ cup freshly grated Parmesan cheese

1 bunch fresh basil leaves

½ cup olive oil

5 cloves garlic, minced

2 tablespoons pine nuts

½ teaspoon salt

For the soup:

3 10½-ounce cans of consommé

1 cup chopped walnuts

Parsley, for garnish

THE COUNTDOWN

One day ahead:

1. Make the pesto, buy it or defrost it.
2. To make it: Grate the Parmesan in the food processor. Add the rest of the pesto ingredients blend until smooth. Refrigerate. This recipe makes more than enough for the soup, but you can freeze the rest.
3. Pour the consommé into a sauce pan and add half the amount of water suggested on the can. Stir in at least 2 tablespoons of pesto. Cool, cover and refrigerate.
4. Wash, chop and dry the parsley. Refrigerate in a plastic bag.

Fifteen minutes before your guests are expected:

1. Gently heat the soup on the stove.
2. When hot, cover and turn off the heat.

Just before serving:

1. Bring the soup almost to a boil.
2. Place chopped walnuts in each soup cup, add the hot soup and garnish with parsley.

Don't just stand there, say something

Squash Bisque

Serves 6

This is no red-neck soup … it's yellow-neck, subtle, smooth and sophisticated

YOU WILL NEED

1 package frozen butternut or acorn squash

4 yellow-neck squash

4 tablespoons butter

1 tablespoon olive oil

3 leeks, chopped

1 onion, chopped

4 to 5 cups chicken broth

2 tablespoons fresh thyme, minced, or 2 teaspoons dried

Salt and freshly ground pepper

⅓ cup cream (optional)

3 tablespoons chopped chives

THE COUNTDOWN

Two days ahead:

1. Defrost the frozen squash. Preheat the oven to 375°.
2. Wash the yellow-neck squash, slice in ¼-inch slices and set aside.

3. In a Dutch oven, heat the butter and the oil, add the leeks and onion, and sauté until soft. Add the yellow-neck squash, chicken broth and thyme. Bring almost to a boil, reduce the heat and simmer for 25 minutes.

4. In a food processor, purée the yellow-neck squash until smooth. Return to the Dutch oven. Add the butternut squash and more broth if needed. Season with salt and pepper to taste. Cover and refrigerate.

At least an hour before your guests are expected:

1. Remove the soup from the refrigerator.

Forty-five minutes before:

1. Gently heat the soup. Cover and turn the heat off

Just before serving:

1. Bring to piping hot, adding cream if desired.

2. Sprinkle chives on top.

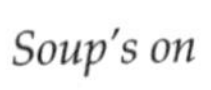

Soup's on

Tango Soup

Serves 6

This dance of tomatoes and sweet potatoes is irresistible

YOU WILL NEED

1 tablespoon butter

1 tablespoon olive oil

1 large onion, finely chopped

1 stalk celery, finely chopped

2 cloves garlic, minced

1 carrot, finely chopped

2 medium sweet potatoes, peeled and chopped

1 16-ounce can stewed tomatoes

4 cups chicken broth

1 teaspoon sugar

¼ teaspoon nutmeg

½ teaspoon ground ginger

Salt and freshly ground pepper

Parsley, for garnish

THE COUNTDOWN

One or two days ahead:

1. Heat the butter and the oil in a medium pot. Sauté the chopped onion, celery and garlic until the onion is soft.
2. Add the carrot and potatoes to the pot and sauté gently for 5 minutes.
3. Add the tomatoes and 2 cups of the chicken broth. Bring to a boil, cover and cook over low heat until potatoes are *just* tender, approximately 15 minutes.
4. Purée in a food processor. If the soup seems too thick, add more chicken broth and stir well.
5. Add the sugar and the seasonings. Cool, cover and refrigerate.
6. Chop the parsley and refrigerate in a plastic bag.

At least an hour before your guests are expected:

1. Remove the pot from the refrigerator.

Fifteen minutes before:

1. Heat the soup gently, stirring. Adjust the seasonings.
2. Cover and turn off the heat.

Just before serving:

1. Bring the soup to piping hot and ladle into soup bowls.
2. Garnish with parsley.

Salads

Lettuce is like conversation: it must be fresh and crisp.

– Charles Dudley Warner

Artichoke Hearts
with Roasted Pepper Sauce

Serves 6

Move over, Peter Piper

YOU WILL NEED

For the pepper sauce:

2 large red bell peppers

2 cloves garlic, minced

4 tablespoons olive oil

3 tablespoons red wine vinegar

Salt and freshly ground pepper

1 brown paper bag

For the artichokes:

2 14-ounce cans of artichoke hearts

3 cups mixed greens

THE COUNTDOWN

Two days ahead:

1. Lightly oil a baking sheet. Preheat the oven to 500°.
2. Cut each pepper in half lengthwise and remove the stems, seeds and white membranes. Place the pepper halves, cut side down, on the baking sheet and coat lightly with oil.
3. Roast the peppers in the oven until skins darken and blister, 12 to 15 minutes.
4. Place the peppers in a paper bag, close tightly and set aside to steam for about 10 minutes.
5. Take the peppers from the bag and remove the skins.
6. Place the peppers and the rest of the sauce ingredients in a food processor. Purée until smooth, about 1 minute. Place in a small bowl, cover tightly with plastic wrap and refrigerate.

7. Quarter the artichokes and place them in their liquid in the refrigerator, covered.
8. Wash the greens, dry, put into a zippered plastic bag and refrigerate.

At least an hour before your guests are expected:

1. Remove the sauce and the artichokes from the refrigerator. Drain the artichokes and set aside.

Just before serving:

1. Arrange greens on each plate and drizzle on a little pepper sauce.
2. Scatter artichokes on top and spoon more sauce over them.

Asparagus with Nutty Vinaigrette

Serves 6

Not just any old green vegetable, this is company *green*

YOU WILL NEED

For the vinaigrette:

1/3 cup hazelnuts or walnuts

3 scallions, finely chopped

1 shallot, finely chopped

2 tablespoons red wine vinegar

1 tablespoon Dijon mustard

½ teaspoon sugar

1/3 cup olive oil

For the asparagus:

2¼ pounds asparagus, or about 42 spears

6 thin slices of lemon for garnish

6 sprigs of parsley for garnish

The higher your income, the higher you cut

THE COUNTDOWN

One day ahead:

1. Preheat the oven to 350°.
2. Place the nuts in a shallow ovenproof dish or on a baking sheet and toast until lightly browned. Watch carefully to avoid burning. If you use hazelnuts, wrap the hot nuts in a dish towel and rub them together to remove the skins. When cool, chop the nuts.
3. Whisk together the rest of the vinaigrette ingredients and stir in the nuts. Set aside in a cool place.
4. Rinse the asparagus. Break at least an inch off the bottoms and trim the lower half of the stalks with a carrot peeler.
5. In a large skillet bring to a boil enough salted water to cover the asparagus and cook it until a fork just penetrates the thickest part of the stems, from 2 to 5 minutes. Drain carefully in a colander and spread the spears out on a paper towel to cool quickly and keep their color.
6. When cool enough to handle, place the asparagus in a baking dish and add a little vinaigrette. Wrap plastic tightly over the asparagus and then wrap more plastic over the dish. Refrigerate.
7. Thinly slice the lemons. Wrap in plastic and refrigerate.
8. Wash the parsley sprigs, dry, place in a plastic bag and refrigerate.

At least an hour before your guests are expected:

1. Remove the asparagus, vinaigrette, lemon slices and parsley from the refrigerator.

Just before serving:

1. Whisk the vinaigrette and drizzle over the asparagus. Turn the asparagus and add a little more vinaigrette if necessary.
2. Place a portion of asparagus on each plate and garnish with a lemon slice and a sprig of parsley.

Celery Root & Beets
with Apple Vinaigrette

Serves 6

You don't have to root for these roots—this recipe will make your culinary reputation

YOU WILL NEED

3 medium beets

1 large bulb of celery root (celeriac)

For the sauce:

¼ cup chopped walnuts

1 Granny Smith apple, peeled and coarsely chopped

¼ cup apple cider vinegar

¼ cup apple juice

1 garlic clove, minced

1 tablespoon grainy mustard

1 cup canola or other light oil

Salt and freshly ground pepper

For the garnish:

Chives, chopped

1 cup chopped walnuts, toasted

THE COUNTDOWN

Two days ahead:

1. Place the beets in a saucepan, cover with water and bring to a boil. Cook until just tender, about 45 minutes. Drain, cool and peel.
2. Peel the celery root and shred, either with a hand grater or in a food processor. Measure 1½ cups into in a bowl and refrigerate.
3. Shred the beets, place 1½ cups in a separate bowl and refrigerate.

One day ahead:

1. In a blender, combine the walnuts, apple, vinegar, apple juice, garlic and mustard. Turn on the blender and slowly pour in the oil. When well mixed, season with salt and pepper and refrigerate.
2. Chop the chives and refrigerate in a plastic bag.

An hour before your guests are expected:

1. Remove the celery root, beets, chives and vinaigrette from the refrigerator. Lightly mix vinaigrette separately with the beets and then with the celery, using half to two thirds of the vinaigrette.
2. Toast the walnuts until lightly browned. Set aside.

Just before serving:

1. Place a portion of beets in the center of each plate and surround with celery root.
2. Sprinkle walnuts and chives over all.

I don't want to be late . . .

Danish Blue Cheese Mousse

Serves 6

This has real cachet

YOU WILL NEED

¼ cup cold water

1 tablespoon gelatin

1 teaspoon cognac

½ teaspoon Worcestershire sauce

½ cup heavy cream

1 tablespoon minced onion

6 ounces Danish blue cheese

6 ounces cream cheese

Salt and freshly ground pepper

2 tablespoons chopped chives

Lettuce

THE COUNTDOWN

Two days ahead:

1. Pour the water into a small saucepan and sprinkle the gelatin on top. When gelatin has softened, turn on the heat to dissolve it. When dissolved, turn the heat off again and allow to cool slightly.
2. In a blender combine the gelatin liquid, cognac, Worcestershire sauce, cream and minced onion. Blend.
3. Add half the blue cheese and blend. Add the rest of the blue cheese and blend again.
4. Add half the cream cheese and blend. Add the rest of the cream cheese and blend again.
5. Add pepper and the chives. Blend. Add salt if necessary.
6. Pour the mixture into an 8-inch glass pie dish, cover and refrigerate.

7. Wash and dry the lettuce, put in a zippered plastic bag and refrigerate.

One day ahead:

1. Take the mousse from the refrigerator and slide a hot knife around the edge.
2. Warm the bottom of the dish in hot water for a few seconds to loosen, then tip the mousse onto a plate.
3. Cover and return to the refrigerator.

Thirty minutes before your guests are expected:

1. Arrange lettuce leaves on each plate.
2. Lay thin wedges of mousse on top.

Honey, the mousse jelled!

Eggplant Rollups
with Herbed Cheese

Serves 6

Eggplant has never been treated so well

YOU WILL NEED

For the eggplant:

6 ounces Boursin cheese

1 medium to large eggplant, peeled

1 teaspoon salt

½ tablespoon olive oil

For the marinade:

¼ cup red wine vinegar

½ cup olive oil

1 garlic clove, minced

¼ tablespoon of tarragon

¼ tablespoon of chives

Salt and freshly ground pepper

6 rather large lettuce leaves

Chopped parsley for garnish

THE COUNTDOWN

One or two days ahead:

1. Remove the cheese from the refrigerator.
2. Cut the eggplant the long way into one-third-inch slices. Place in a colander, sprinkle with salt and let drain for about 30 minutes.
3. Combine the marinade ingredients in a bowl, whisk and set aside.
4. Dry the eggplant with paper towels.
5. Preheat the oven to 375°.
6. Line a cookie sheet with heavy foil. Oil the foil.
7. Brush both sides of the eggplant slices with oil, lay them on the baking sheet and bake for 6 minutes.

8. Turn the slices over and continue baking until they are pliable enough to roll, 4 to 8 minutes. Loosen the slices and let them cool on the sheet.
9. Spread cheese on each eggplant slice. Roll the slices up the long way and place in a single layer, seam side down, in a shallow baking dish.
10. Stir the marinade and pour over the eggplant rolls, cover tightly and refrigerate.

An hour before your guests are expected:

1. Remove the eggplant rollups from the refrigerator.
2. Slice each one into 3 pieces.

Just before serving:

1. Place a lettuce leaf on each plate, sprinkle with a little marinade, and place three pieces of eggplant roll on each leaf.
2. Spoon a little more marinade over all and sprinkle parsley on top.

Goat Cheese & Sun-Dried Tomatoes on Red-Leaf Lettuce

Serves 6

Great combo

YOU WILL NEED

3 tablespoons balsamic vinegar

2 garlic cloves, minced

Salt and freshly ground pepper

5 tablespoons olive oil

12 sun-dried tomatoes

3 ounces fresh goat cheese, crumbled

12 red-leaf lettuce leaves

THE COUNTDOWN

Two days ahead:

1. Combine the vinegar, garlic, salt and pepper. Slowly whisk in the olive oil. Refrigerate in a covered jar.
2. Drain and coarsely chop the sun-dried tomatoes. Refrigerate in a covered jar.
3. Crumble the goat cheese, place in plastic bag and refrigerate.

One day ahead:

1. Wash the lettuce, dry, tear into bite-sized pieces and refrigerate.

At least an hour before:

1. Remove the vinaigrette, tomatoes and goat cheese from the refrigerator.

Just before serving:

1. Place a portion of red-leaf lettuce on each plate and sprinkle vinaigrette over it.
2. Scatter tomatoes and goat cheese on top. Sprinkle a little more vinaigrette over all.

More vinegar, methinks

Green Beans with Pecan Sauce

Serves 6

It's not true that if you've seen one bean you've seen them all. Not these green beans, anyway

YOU WILL NEED

1 cup chopped pecans

1 garlic clove, minced

3 tablespoons chopped cilantro, or 1 teaspoon ground coriander

1½ teaspoons paprika

Salt and freshly ground pepper

¼ cup red wine vinegar

¼ cup, or more, chicken broth

1½ pounds green beans

1 small red onion

Fresh dill, for garnish

THE COUNTDOWN

One day ahead:

1. Toast the pecans. In a food processor, purée the pecans, garlic, cilantro/coriander, paprika, salt and pepper, vinegar, and enough chicken broth to make a smooth paste. Cover and refrigerate.
2. Trim the beans, place in boiling salted water in a large skillet and cook until crisp-tender, 4 to 6 minutes depending on the size of the beans. You must check them continually.
3. Rinse in cold water, drain and dry. Cut the beans in half crosswise. Wrap in plastic and refrigerate.
4. Peel and thinly slice the red onion. Wrap and refrigerate.
5. Wash the dill, dry, snip and refrigerate in a plastic bag.

At least an hour before your guests are expected:

1. Remove the beans, onion slices and pecan sauce from the refrigerator.

2. You may want to add a little more chicken broth to the sauce.

Just before serving:

1. Place a portion of the beans on each plate and scatter onions on top.
2. Add a generous portion of pecan sauce. Garnish with snipped dill.

Leek and Red Pepper Salad

Serves 6

It looks as good as it tastes, and that's saying a mouthful

YOU WILL NEED

For the salad:

6 leeks

3 large red bell peppers

1 bunch scallions

1 stalk celery

1 small red onion

Lettuce

For the vinaigrette

3 tablespoons lemon juice

2 cloves garlic, minced

1 teaspoon dry mustard

½ teaspoon dried dill

¾ cup olive oil

Salt and freshly ground pepper

THE COUNTDOWN

One day ahead:

1. Wash the leeks and slice lengthwise. Cut peppers into ¼-inch strips. Chop the scallions. Finely chop the celery and the onions.
2. Steam the leeks and the peppers for about 5 minutes. Steam the scallions for about 2 minutes. Drain, cool, cover and refrigerate.
3. Finely chop the celery and the onion. Refrigerate in a plastic bag.
4. Whisk together the ingredients for the vinaigrette. Refrigerate in a covered jar.

Just before serving:

1. Arrange a lettuce leaf or two on each plate, place the leeks and peppers carefully on top.
2. Sprinkle the salad with celery and onions, then drizzle the vinaigrette over all.

Mushrooms & Roasted Red Peppers
with Balsamic Vinaigrette

Serves 6

A new high for the lowly white mushroom

YOU WILL NEED

For the vinaigrette:

1/3 cup balsamic vinegar

1 large garlic clove, minced

Salt and freshly ground pepper

1/3 cup olive oil

For the salad:

2 red bell peppers

1½ pounds of white mushrooms

4 handfuls of arugula or spinach

12 black olives

THE COUNTDOWN

One or two days ahead:

1. Preheat the oven to 500°. Lightly oil a baking sheet.
2. Make the vinaigrette: Combine the vinegar, garlic, salt and pepper. Slowly whisk in the oil.
3. Cut each pepper in half lengthwise and remove the stems, seeds and white membranes.
4. Place the pepper halves, cut side down, on the oiled baking sheet and coat lightly with oil.

5. Roast the peppers in the oven until the skins darken and blister, 12 to 15 minutes. Place the peppers in a paper bag, close tightly and set aside to steam for about 10 minutes.
6. Take the peppers from the bag, remove the skins and slice into wide strips.
7. Remove and discard the mushroom stems. Wipe the caps with a damp paper towel and cut in half.
8. Reserve 3 tablespoons of vinaigrette. Toss the rest with the pepper strips and mushrooms.
9. Wash the greens, dry, put in a zippered plastic bag and refrigerate.
10. Halve the olives and refrigerate.
11. Stir the mushroom-pepper mixture once or twice in the next day or two.

The tranquil cook

An hour before your guests are expected:

1. Remove the mushroom-pepper mixture and the reserved vinaigrette from the refrigerator.

Just before serving:

1. Place a portion of greens on each plate and sprinkle with a little of the reserved vinaigrette.
2. Place a portion of mushrooms and peppers on top and garnish with the sliced olives.

Mushrooms on Spinach with Shaved Parmesan

Serves 6

A most satisfying salad and a great first course

YOU WILL NEED

1 pound fresh mushrooms

Juice of 2 lemons

1½ pounds fresh spinach leaves

½ pound solid Parmesan cheese

4 to 5 tablespoons olive oil

Salt and freshly ground pepper

THE COUNTDOWN

One day ahead:

1. Wipe the mushrooms clean with a damp towel. Discard the stems and cut into thin slices.
2. Place the slices in a bowl, coat them thoroughly with lemon juice, cover and refrigerate.
3. Wash the spinach leaves, removing tough stems. Dry, place in a zippered plastic bag and refrigerate.
4. Shave the Parmesan cheese with a carrot peeler, place the shavings in a plastic bag and refrigerate.

An hour before your guests are expected:

1. Take the mushrooms from the refrigerator. Pour off and save the lemon juice.

2. Add the Parmesan shavings to the mushrooms and toss with olive oil, salt and pepper. Taste and add more lemon juice if desired.

Just before serving:

1. Sprinkle the spinach leaves with olive oil and arrange on the plates.
2. Place a portion of the mushroom and Parmesan mixture on the spinach leaves.

Prosciutto and Cashew Nut Salad

Serves 6

A combination that sings

YOU WILL NEED

2 tablespoons fresh lemon juice

1½ tablespoons balsamic vinegar

1 tablespoon minced shallot

1 large garlic clove, minced

1 teaspoon salt

Freshly ground pepper

Scant ½ cup olive oil

2 heads Bibb lettuce

1 bunch scallions

6 slices prosciutto, thinly sliced

1 cup halved cashew nuts

6 ounces fresh goat cheese

THE COUNTDOWN

One or two days ahead:

1. Whisk together the lemon juice, vinegar, shallot, garlic, salt and pepper. Gradually whisk in the oil. Refrigerate in a covered jar.
2. Wash the greens, dry, place in a plastic bag and refrigerate.
3. Slice the scallions. Tear the prosciutto into small pieces. Refrigerate in separate plastic bags.

At least an hour before your guests are expected:

1. Toast the cashews until lightly browned. Crumble the cheese. Set aside.
2. Place the salad greens in a bowl and add the scallions and the prosciutto. Mix gently and return to the refrigerator.
3. Remove the vinaigrette from the refrigerator.

Just before serving:

1. Shake the salad dressing, sprinkle a little over the salad and toss.
2. Add the toasted cashews and the goat cheese, drizzle on a little more dressing and toss again. Arrange a serving on each plate.

Prosciutto? You've come a long way, little pig

Salmon Mounds on Mixed Greens

Serves 6

Rich and rewarding. Fit for any kings and queens who might drop by

YOU WILL NEED

¼ cup olive oil

2 tablespoons lemon juice

1 15-ounce can salmon

Salt and freshly ground pepper

1 cup heavy cream

3 cups mixed greens

6 large black olives

Parsley for garnish

THE COUNTDOWN

One day ahead:

1. Mix the olive oil and lemon juice in a bowl.
2. Drain the salmon removing any bones or skin. Crumble into the bowl. Add the salt and pepper. Using a fork and spoon, mix well.
3. Whip the cream until it is stiff. Gently fold the cream into the salmon mixture. Refrigerate.
4. Wash the greens, dry, place in a plastic bag and refrigerate.
5. Slice the olives and chop the parsley. Cover separately and refrigerate.

Just before serving:

1. Place a serving of greens on each plate and spoon a mound of salmon on top.
2. Garnish with sliced black olives and parsley.

Scallops on a Bed of Celery

Serves 6

In looks, taste, and texture, this is a grand beginning to a meal

YOU WILL NEED

1¼ pounds sea scallops

½ cup freshly squeezed lime juice

¾ cup water

¾ cup white wine

1 large bunch of celery

6 large Boston lettuce leaves

Cilantro, chopped for garnish

For the vinaigrette

2 tablespoons wine vinegar

½ tablespoon Dijon mustard

½ cup olive oil

Salt and freshly ground pepper

THE COUNTDOWN

One day ahead:

1. Quarter the scallops.
2. In a medium saucepan, bring the lime juice, water and wine to a boil.
3. Turn off the heat, *immediately* add the scallops (add boiling water if needed to cover) and remove from the stove to cool.
4. When cool, cover and refrigerate.
5. Wash the celery, remove the strings, and chop the stalks and the tender leaves. Dry, place in a plastic bag and refrigerate.
6. Separate the lettuce leaves from the head, wash, dry and refrigerate in a zippered plastic bag. Chop the cilantro, place in a plastic bag and refrigerate.
7. Combine the ingredients for the vinaigrette, place in a covered jar and refrigerate.

An hour before your guests are expected:

1. Remove the vinaigrette from the refrigerator.

Fifteen minutes before:

1. Remove the scallops and celery from the refrigerator.
2. Arrange lettuce, celery and celery leaves on six salad plates.

Just before serving:

1. Shake the vinaigrette and sprinkle a little over the celery and lettuce.
2. Drain the scallops and apportion them on the celery.
3. Sprinkle vinaigrette and cilantro over all.

Shrimp Salad
with Olives, Celery and Snow Peas

Serves 6

An eye-catcher, a taste-catcher — what more can anyone ask?

YOU WILL NEED

For the salad:

½ cup white wine

2 teaspoons salt

1 pound (24 to 26) shrimp

½ pound snow peas

4 celery stalks

2 bunches scallions

5 cups mixed greens, bite size

12 black olives, sliced

Flat-leafed parsley, chopped fine for garnish

For the dressing:

5 tablespoons mayonnaise

5 tablespoons white wine vinegar

1¾ tablespoons water

5 tablespoons olive oil

1 tablespoon grated fresh ginger

Salt and freshly ground pepper

Almost always

THE COUNTDOWN

One day ahead:

1. In a medium saucepan put 3 quarts of water, the wine and the salt. Bring to a rolling boil.
2. Add the shrimp and lower the heat. When the shrimp turn pink, take them from the stove and drain. Cool, shell, cover and refrigerate in the coldest part of the refrigerator.
3. Wash the snow peas and remove tips and strings. Steam for one minute, cool and refrigerate.

4. Rinse, string and coarsely chop the celery. Refrigerate.
5. Rinse and chop the scallions, using part of the green tops. Refrigerate.
6. Wash and dry the mixed greens. Refrigerate.
7. Drain the olives, cut in half and refrigerate.
8. Wash and dry the parsley, chop and refrigerate.
9. Mix the mayonnaise, vinegar and water in a small bowl. Slowly whisk in the olive oil and add the grated ginger. Add salt and pepper to taste. Refrigerate.

Thirty minutes before your guests are expected:

1. Take the dressing from the refrigerator.
2. Take out the snow peas, celery, scallions and greens. Toss them together in a bowl.

Just before serving:

1. Take the shrimp from the refrigerator, place them in the bowl with the greens and vegetables and toss with some of the dressing (you may not need all of it).
2. Arrange a portion of salad on each plate. Scatter olives and parsley on top.

A long-term relationship

Sliced Cucumbers
with Orange-Grapefruit Dressing

Serves 6

When the ordinary becomes extraordinarily tasty

YOU WILL NEED

For the dressing:

- Rind of one orange, grated
- 2 tablespoons fresh orange juice
- 2 tablespoons unsweetened grapefruit juice
- Juice of ½ lemon
- 1 tablespoon white wine vinegar
- 1 teaspoon cider vinegar
- ¼ cup light olive oil
- Salt and freshly ground pepper
- Pinch of sugar

For the salad:

- 4 cups of green and red lettuce
- 1 red onion
- 3 medium-sized cucumbers
- 1 10-ounce package frozen green peas

THE COUNTDOWN

One day ahead:

1. Grate the orange rind, place in a plastic bag and refrigerate.
2. In a small bowl mix the fruit juices, the lemon juice and the two vinegars. Slowly whisk the olive oil into the mixture. Add salt and pepper to taste and a little sugar if the dressing is too sharp. Refrigerate.
3. Wash the lettuce, dry, place in a zippered plastic bag and refrigerate.
4. Thinly slice the red onion and refrigerate.
5. Slice the cucumbers paper thin, place in a bowl of salted ice-water and refrigerate.

At least an hour before your guests are expected:

1. Defrost the frozen peas.
2. Drain the cucumbers and return them, covered, to the refrigerator.
3. Remove the dressing and the onions from the refrigerator.

Just before serving:

1. Place lettuce leaves on each plate. Scatter cucumber slices, red onion slices and green peas on the lettuce.
2. Whisk the dressing and drizzle onto the salad.
3. Sprinkle the grated orange rind on top and serve.

Beef & Veal Entrées

The winter evening settles down
with smell of steaks in passageways.
Six o'clock.

– T. S. Eliot

Beef with Almonds & Apricots

Serves 6

An elegant entrée—be prepared for rave reviews

YOU WILL NEED

½ pound dried apricots

1½ cups boiling water

Salt and pepper

¾ teaspoon cinnamon

3 pounds sirloin tip, cut into 1" cubes

½ cup olive oil

2 large onions, chopped

6 garlic cloves, minced

1 teaspoon ground coriander

¼ teaspoon ground cloves

2 teaspoons ground cumin

½ cup dry white wine

2 cups canned whole tomatoes

3½ cups beef broth

½ cup raisins

2 tablespoons Italian parsley

¾ cup slivered almonds

Rice for 6 to 8 servings

THE COUNTDOWN

One or two days ahead:

1. Plump the apricots in the boiling water.
2. Mix the salt, pepper and cinnamon and toss with the beef cubes.
3. Pour 4 tablespoons of the oil into a heavy pan and heat until almost smoking. Add a layer of beef cubes and sauté over high heat. When well-browned on all sides, transfer to a bowl with a slotted spoon. Brown the remaining beef cubes, adding more oil if needed, and put into the bowl.
4. Pour the rest of the oil into the heavy pan. Add the onions and cook over moderate heat until softened, about 10 minutes. Add garlic, coriander, cloves and cumin. Cook, stirring, for 3 minutes. Add wine and cook 2 minutes longer.

5. Mash the tomatoes with a spoon and add with their liquid to the sauce. Stir in the beef broth.
6. Drain the apricots, set aside 12 for garnish and add the rest to the sauce. Bring almost to a boil and simmer for 2 minutes.
7. In a food processor, purée the sauce until smooth. Pour into a large Dutch oven and add the beef. Bring just to a boil, then lower the heat, cover and cook for about 1¾ hours, stirring occasionally.
8. Remove the cover and simmer until the meat is very tender and the sauce is thick, 20 to 30 minutes. Add the raisins, season with salt and pepper, cool, cover and refrigerate.
9. Chop the reserved apricots and the parsley. Refrigerate.

Suggested Menu

Danish Blue Cheese Mousse

Beef with Almonds & Apricots

Wine Red Jelly

At least an hour before your guests are expected:

1. Remove the beef, apricots and parsley from the refrigerator.
2. Toast the almonds until lightly browned. Set aside.

At least forty-five minutes before:

1. Cook the rice, cover and keep warm.
2. Put the pot of beef on the stove, cover and reheat, stirring occasionally. When hot, turn off the heat.

Just before serving:

1. Heat the beef to piping hot. Place a portion of rice in the center of each plate and top with a portion of beef.
2. Sprinkle the almonds, reserved apricots and parsley over all.

Beef with a Southern Accent

Serves 6

This combination of ingredients pleases the palate and comforts the soul. Y'all enjoy

YOU WILL NEED

3 tablespoons vegetable oil
3 tablespoons unsalted butter
3 pounds boneless chuck, in 1″ cubes
4 medium onions, chopped
½ teaspoon dried thyme
¼ teaspoon ground cinnamon
½ teaspoon ground cloves
2 tablespoons flour
1 tablespoon catsup
1 bay leaf
2 teaspoons salt
½ teaspoon pepper
1 teaspoon grated lemon peel
1½ cups dry white wine
1 29-ounce can pear halves
4 medium sweet potatoes
3 tablespoons seedless raisins,
Chopped parsley for garnish

THE COUNTDOWN:

One or two days ahead:

1. In a large skillet heat the oil and butter. Without crowding, brown the beef cubes on all sides. Remove from the skillet and set aside.
2. Add the onions, thyme, cinnamon and cloves to the drippings in the skillet and sauté until tender, about 5 minutes, adding more oil if necessary.
3. Turn off the heat. Mix in the flour, catsup, bay leaf, salt, pepper, and grated lemon peel. Slowly stir in the wine.
4. Setting the pears aside, pour their syrup into the skillet and add the browned beef cubes.

5. Bring to a boil. Cover, turn down the heat and simmer gently until the meat is tender, about an hour and twenty minutes. Cool.
6. Boil the sweet potatoes gently in their skins until *just* tender, checking frequently to avoid overcooking. Drain immediately, cool and peel. Cut each potato lengthwise into 4 slices.
7. Plump the raisins in hot water. Drain.
8. In a large shallow baking dish, distribute evenly the sweet potato slices, pear halves and raisins. Spoon beef and sauce over all, cover and refrigerate.

Suggested Menu

Celery Root & Beets with Apple Vinaigrette

Beef with a Southern Accent

Savannah Orange Pie

At least an hour before your guests are expected:

1. Take the baking dish from the refrigerator and preheat the oven to 350°.

Forty-five minutes before:

1. Cover the baking dish and place in the oven until thoroughly heated, 25 to 35 minutes. Turn off the oven and keep warm.

Just before serving:

1. Place a portion of beef on each dinner plate.
2. Carefully place several slices of sweet potato and half a pear next to the meat.
3. Garnish with parsley.

Is that the doorbell?

Steak Salad
with Roquefort Dressing

Serves 6

Lovely on a warm summer evening
or serve with a hot soup on cooler days

YOU WILL NEED

For the marinade:

1 cup dry red wine

½ cup olive oil

2 scallions, minced

3 garlic cloves, minced

1 teaspoon salt

½ teaspoon freshly ground pepper

1½ teaspoons dry mustard

2 bay leaves, crushed

For the steak:

2 pounds sirloin steak, 1″ thick

For the salad:

Mixed salad greens

5 stalks celery

For the salad dressing:

¾ cup mayonnaise

¾ cup sour cream

3 tablespoons white vinegar

6 ounces Roquefort cheese, crumbled

Salt and freshly ground pepper

Loaf of French bread

THE COUNTDOWN

Two days ahead:

1. Combine the marinade ingredients.
2. Prick the steak with a fork and put it, with the marinade, into a zippered plastic bag. Squeeze the air from the bag, close and refrigerate.

One day ahead:

1. Wash the salad greens, dry, place in a plastic bag and refrigerate.
2. Chop the celery and refrigerate.
3. Mix salad dressing ingredients and refrigerate.
4. Remove the steak from the marinade. In a non-stick skillet, over high heat, sear the steak on both sides. Reduce the heat and cook for approximately 4 minutes per side for medium-rare (grill the steak if you prefer). Cool, cover tightly and refrigerate.

Suggested Menu

Gazpacho

Steak Salad with Roquefort Dressing

Bronzy Bananas & Apricots

At least an hour before your guests are expected:

1. Remove the salad dressing from the refrigerator.
2. Remove the steak from the refrigerator and carve into thin slices.

Fifteen minutes before:

1. Place a handful of greens and a handful of celery on each plate.
2. Arrange steak slices on top and add a large spoonful of the dressing.
3. Put the rest of the dressing in a bowl and pass.

Serve: With French bread

Veal Estouffade
with Potato Gratin

Serves 6

A word to the wise: try this sage stew

YOU WILL NEED

For the veal:

¼ cup olive oil

4 tablespoons butter

2 pounds of veal shoulder, cut into 1″ cubes

12 garlic cloves, peeled

1 pound portobello and white mushrooms, mixed

2 cups white wine

2 tablespoons flour

1 cup chicken broth

½ cup fresh sage

¼ cup fresh Italian parsley, chopped

¼ cup apricot brandy

Grated zest of 1 medium orange

Salt and pepper

1 heaping tablespoon red currant jelly

Chopped parsley for garnish

For the potatoes:

1 tablespoon of ground cumin

1 teaspoon ground turmeric

A pinch of cayenne pepper

1½ teaspoons salt

Freshly ground pepper

2 garlic cloves, minced

1 tablespoon unsalted butter

2 large onions

3 large baking potatoes

1 cup heavy cream

THE COUNTDOWN

Two days ahead:

1. Preheat the oven to 350°.
2. Put the oil and 1 tablespoon of the butter in a Dutch oven. Turn heat to high.
3. Brown the veal, a few pieces at a time. When brown on all sides, remove with a slotted spoon and set aside.
4. Sauté the garlic in the Dutch oven and add to the veal. Discard the oil and butter in the skillet.
5. Put the remaining 3 tablespoons of butter in the Dutch oven and scrape up any browned bits. Add the mushrooms and cook rapidly over high heat, stirring constantly, for 1 to 2 minutes. Add 1 cup of the wine and bring to a boil.
6. Sprinkle flour over the veal and garlic. Put into the Dutch oven and add the second cup of wine, the chicken broth, the sage, parsley, brandy and orange zest. Stir well. Add salt and pepper to taste.
7. Cover and bake for 40 minutes.
8. Remove from the oven, cool and refrigerate.

Suggested Menu

Asparagus with Nutty Vinaigrette

Veal Estouffade with Potato Gratin

Mocha Crème Brulée

One day ahead:

1. Preheat the oven to 350°. Butter a large baking dish.
2. In a small bowl, stir together the cumin, turmeric, salt and pepper. Add the garlic and stir again.
3. Peal the potatoes and slice very thin. Arrange half the potatoes in a single layer in the buttered baking dish, overlapping a little. Sprinkle half the spice mixture over the potatoes.
4. Chop the onions and put into the dish with the remaining potatoes. Sprinkle on the rest of the spices and pour the cream over all.
5. Cover with foil and bake until the potatoes are just crisp-tender, 50 to 60 minutes. Cool and refrigerate.

Forty-five minutes before your guests are expected:

1. Remove the veal and the potatoes from the refrigerator and uncover.
2. Preheat the oven to 325°.

Thirty minutes before:

1. Gently reheat the veal for approximately 30 minutes. Put the dish of potatoes in the oven for the last 15 minutes.
2. When hot, cover both dishes, leave them in the oven and turn off the heat.

Just before serving:

1. Stir the jelly into the veal until dissolved.
2. Place a portion of veal and a portion of potatoes on each dinner plate.
3. Sprinkle parsley over all.

Lamb Entrées

. . . that wonderful little lamb stew I had the other night. . . . It was so wonderful you could cuddle it in your arms.

– James Beard

Braised Lamb Shanks
with White Beans

Serves 6

"Thanks for the shanks," cried the guests

YOU WILL NEED

For the shanks:

6 lamb shanks, trimmed of excess fat and cut in half crosswise by the butcher

Kosher salt and freshly ground pepper

3 tablespoons olive oil

12 garlic cloves, minced

1 large onion, chopped

4 cups red wine

5 cups chicken broth

1½ tablespoons tomato paste

1 cinnamon stick

2 bay leaves

3 teaspoons dried rosemary, crumbled

Parsley sprigs for garnish

For the beans:

4 15-ounce cans small white beans

1½ pounds pearl onions

1 tablespoon butter

4 garlic cloves, minced

¼ cup red wine

½ cup chicken broth

½ cup chopped parsley

Salt and pepper to taste

THE COUNTDOWN

Two or three days ahead:

1. Preheat the oven to 350°. Coat the lamb with salt and pepper.
2. In a large roasting pan on top of the stove, heat the oil and brown the shanks on all sides. Remove and set aside.
3. In the same pan, sauté the garlic and onion until soft. Add the wine and simmer until the liquid is reduced by one-third.

4. Add 4 cups of the chicken broth, tomato paste, cinnamon stick, bay leaves and rosemary. Stir.
5. Add the shanks, cover the pan with foil and place in the oven for two hours, basting frequently.
6. Remove from the oven, cool, cover and refrigerate.

Suggested Menu

Salmon Mounds on Mixed Greens

Braised Lamb Shanks with White Beans

Pears in Red Wine

One day ahead:

1. Thoroughly rinse the beans in a colander. Set aside.
2. In a large stew pot, bring to a boil enough water to blanch the onions for 10 minutes. Drain, cool and peel.
3. In the same pot, sauté the minced garlic, add the red wine and chicken broth. Simmer a few minutes and cool. Add the beans and onions, cover and refrigerate.
4. Chop the parsley and refrigerate.

At least an hour before your guests are expected:

1. Remove the shanks and the bean mixture from the refrigerator and preheat the oven to 350°.

An hour before:

1. Pour the remaining cup of chicken broth over the shanks, cover and place in the oven for 45 to 50 minutes or until the shanks are heated through.
2. When hot, turn the oven down to 200°.
3. Gently heat the bean mixture on the stove, cover and turn off the heat.

Just before serving:

1. Place a serving of beans and two pieces of lamb shank on each plate
2. Spoon sauce over the meat. Top with sprigs of parsley.

Lamb Chops & Feta Cheese
with Rosemary Potatoes

Serves 6

Juicy and succulent—and needs no tending

YOU WILL NEED

For the lamb chops:

2 onions

6 scallions

4 tablespoons olive oil

3 tomatoes

Salt and pepper

12 loin lamb chops

6 squares of aluminum foil, 12" x 14"

6 tablespoons lemon juice

6 tablespoons parsley, chopped

4 teaspoons oregano leaves, crushed

½ pound feta cheese, crumbled

For the potatoes:

18 small red potatoes

3 tablespoons olive oil

Kosher salt to taste

Freshly ground pepper

1 tablespoon dried rosemary

Parsley, chopped for garnish

THE COUNTDOWN

One day ahead:

1. Chop the onions and the scallions. In a large skillet, sauté in olive oil until tender, about 5 minutes.
2. Chop the tomatoes. Add them to the skillet, season with salt and pepper and simmer for a few minutes. Cool.
3. Lay 2 lamb chops on a square of foil and put a portion of the tomato mixture on top of each chop.

4. Sprinkle with lemon juice, parsley, oregano and feta cheese.
5. Wrap the foil tightly around each pair of chops, place in a shallow baking dish and refrigerate.
6. Oil a roasting pan. Wash and dry the potatoes. Halve them, brush with oil and place them in the pan in a single layer, cut side down. Sprinkle with salt, pepper and rosemary, cover tightly with foil and refrigerate.

Suggested Menu

Green Beans with Pecan Sauce

Lamb Chops with Feta Cheese & Rosemary Potatoes

Chocolate Brandy Pudding Cake

At least an hour before your guests are expected:

1. Preheat the oven to 350°. Take the packets of chops and the pan of potatoes from the refrigerator.

One hour before:

1. Place the packets in the oven on a baking sheet and bake for 1 hour.

Thirty minutes before:

1. Put the potatoes in the oven for 30 minutes.
2. Turn off the oven.

Just before serving:

1. Place one foil packet on each plate and fold back the foil.
2. Surround with potatoes and sprinkle with parsley.

What time did they say?

Lamb Bombay

Serves 6

A sophisticated version of lamb curry

YOU WILL NEED

For the spice mixture:

1 teaspoon each ground cinnamon, nutmeg, cloves

2 teaspoons each ground cardamom, black pepper

4 teaspoons cumin

5 teaspoons ground coriander

For the lamb and sauce:

2 tart apples, cored, peeled and chopped

2 large onions, chopped

⅓ cup unsalted butter

2 tablespoons curry powder

2 pounds boneless leg of lamb, trimmed and cut into 1-inch pieces

1 13-ounce can plum tomatoes, with their juice

¾ cup golden raisins

1 teaspoon red pepper flakes

Salt and pepper

1 tablespoon lemon juice

Rice for six generous servings

For the condiments:

2 avocados, peeled, pitted, and cubed

1 tablespoon lemon juice

2 peppers, green and red, chopped

2 bunches of scallions, chopped

1 cup dry roasted peanuts

1 jar chutney

2 fresh plum tomatoes

2 navel oranges

THE COUNTDOWN

Two or three days ahead:

1. Combine the ingredients for the spice mixture. This will make one-third cup (what you don't use will keep in an airtight container).

2. Sauté the apples and onions in the butter over medium heat, stirring until softened. Add the curry and 1 tablespoon of the spice mixture. Cook the mixture for five minutes, stirring.
3. Add the lamb and the rest of the sauce ingredients. Add enough water to cover the mixture by one inch.
4. *Barely* simmer the mixture, partially covered, until the lamb is tender, about 1½ hours.
5. Stir in the lemon juice, salt and pepper to taste. Cool and refrigerate.
6. Chop the peppers and the scallions, refrigerate separately.
7. Skin and chop the tomatoes. Peel the oranges and cut away the sections. Combine in a bowl and refrigerate.

Suggested Menu

Goat Cheese and Sun-Dried Tomatoes on Red-Leaf Lettuce

Lamb Bombay

Gingered Ice Cream with Strawberry-Rhubarb Sauce

At least an hour before your guests are expected:

1. Remove the lamb, the peppers, the scallions and the tomato-orange mixture from the refrigerator. Cook the rice and keep it warm.
2. Peel and slice the avocados. Sprinkle with lemon juice.
3. Place the condiments in small bowls.

Thirty minutes before:

1. Place the lamb in a large skillet, cover and gently heat. When hot, turn off the heat.

Just before serving:

1. Center a helping of rice on each plate and cover with lamb. Pass the bowls of condiments.

Lamb In A Packet
with Skordalia Sauce

Serves 6

A scrumptious dish … and not a pot to wash

YOU WILL NEED

For the marinade:

¼ cup lemon juice

½ cup dry sherry

½ cup olive oil

1 teaspoon oregano

2 large cloves garlic, minced

1 medium onion, sliced

2 tablespoons fresh mint

For the lamb:

1¾ pounds lean, boned lamb, cut into 1″ cubes

For the Skordalia sauce:

3 large potatoes, peeled

1½ cups mayonnaise

9 garlic cloves, minced

3 tablespoons olive oil

3 tablespoons lemon juice

Salt and pepper to taste

For the vegetables:

6 tomato slices, ½″ thick

2 medium potatoes, thinly sliced

2 medium carrots, in thin strips

2 celery stalks, thinly sliced

12 small white onions, cut in half

6 squares of foil, 12″ x 14″

For the cheeses:

6 tablespoons Feta cheese, crumbled

6 tablespoons grated Parmesan

For the seasonings:

2 teaspoons oregano

3 tablespoons lemon juice

3 tablespoons parsley, chopped

Salt and pepper to taste

THE COUNTDOWN

Two days ahead:

1. Combine the marinade ingredients and purée.
2. Place the lamb cubes in a single layer in a large dish and pour the marinade over the lamb. Cover and refrigerate. Turn occasionally.
3. Make the Skordalia sauce: Boil the potatoes and mash by hand. Add the rest of the sauce ingredients, stir well, cover and refrigerate.

One day ahead:

1. Pour the marinade off the lamb and reserve. Brown the lamb in a skillet, without crowding.
2. Prepare the vegetables.
3. Lay out the six foil squares and put a tablespoon of the reserved marinade in the center of each. Add a portion of lamb, vegetables, cheeses and seasonings, in that order, ending with another tablespoon of marinade.
4. Fold up the squares and crimp edges tightly. Place the packets on a plate and refrigerate.

Suggested Menu

Mushrooms on Spinach with Shaved Parmesan

Lamb in a Packet with Skordalia Sauce

Apples Grand Marnier

Where's the Skordalia sauce?

At least an hour before your guests are expected:

1. Remove the lamb packets and the Skordalia sauce from refrigerator. You may wish to moisten the sauce with a little more mayonnaise, oil or lemon juice.
2. Preheat the oven to 375°.

Thirty minutes before:

1. Place the packets on a baking sheet and bake for 1 hour.
2. Turn oven off. The packets will stay warm up to 30 minutes.

To serve:

1. Place an unopened packet on each dinner plate.
2. Pass the Skordalia sauce.

Pork & Ham Entrées

Everything in a pig is good. What ingratitude has permitted his name to become a term of opprobrium?

– *Grimod de la Reynière*

Pork Tenderloins, Chutney Cream
& Artichoke-Lima Bean Salad

Serves 6

This entrée is to "pork 'n beans" what Champagne is to tap water

YOU WILL NEED

For the marinade:

1 cup red wine

4 teaspoons olive oil

½ teaspoon ground cinnamon

½ teaspoon ground cardamom

2 teaspoons coarse salt

2 teaspoons freshly ground black pepper

For the pork:

2 whole pork tenderloins, about 1 pound each

1 jar chutney

⅔ cup sour cream

For the bean salad:

2 packages frozen baby lima beans

1 can artichoke hearts

4 baby carrots

1 can sliced water chestnuts

3 garlic cloves, minced

Parsley sprigs, for garnish

For the lemon vinaigrette:

½ cup olive oil

¼ cup fresh lemon juice

1 teaspoon Dijon mustard

½ teaspoon coarse salt

Freshly ground pepper

2 cloves garlic, minced

Salt and freshly ground pepper

THE COUNTDOWN

One day ahead:

1. Combine the marinade ingredients.
2. Wipe the tenderloins and place in a plastic bag with the marinade. Squeeze out the air, seal the plastic bag and refrigerate.
3. Stir the chutney lightly into the sour cream. Cover and refrigerate.
4. Bring water to a boil, add the limas beans and simmer for 10 minutes. Drain and place in a large bowl.
5. Quarter the artichokes, thinly slice the carrots, drain the water chestnuts and mince the garlic. Combine with the lima beans.
6. Mix the vinaigrette ingredients and stir into the lima bean mixture. Cover and refrigerate.

Suggested Menu

Herbed Tomato Soup

Pork Tenderloins, Chutney Cream & Artichoke-Lima Bean Salad

Fantastic Fruit Compote

At least an hour before your guests are expected:

1. Preheat the oven to 500°. Take the chutney cream and the lima bean salad from the refrigerator.
2. Remove the pork from the plastic bag, reserving the marinade. Place on a baking pan and roast in the oven for 10 minutes. Turn and roast for another 10 minutes. Remove from oven.
3. While the pork is roasting, pour the reserved marinade into a large saucepan, turn up the heat and allow to boil for 2-3 minutes.
4. Cut the pork into half-inch slices and add them to hot marinade. Turn off the heat and cover.

Just before serving:

1. Bring the pork and marinade to piping hot. Place several slices of pork on each plate and spoon chutney cream over them.
2. Add a portion of lima bean salad and garnish with parsley.

Barbecued-Indoors Country Ribs with Potato-Bean Salad

Serves 6

The sauce for the ribs is to die for. But don't bother ... just enjoy it

YOU WILL NEED

For the salad:

9 medium red-skin potatoes

1¼ pounds of green beans

1 red onion, chopped

1 cup fresh dill

For the salad dressing:

⅓ cup balsamic vinegar

2 tablespoons Dijon mustard

Juice of half a lemon

2 garlic cloves, minced

¾ cup olive oil

Salt and freshly ground pepper

For the barbecue sauce:

12 ounces of Marinara sauce

1 cup light brown sugar, packed

1 tablespoon cinnamon

1 teaspoon dry mustard

1 12-ounce can pineapple chunks, with syrup

6 ounces of a seedless berry jam

⅓ cup parsley, finely chopped

For the ribs:

3 pounds country-style pork ribs

THE COUNTDOWN

Two days ahead:

1. Boil the potatoes in their skins until *just* tender. Cool.
2. In a large skillet, bring salted water to a boil. Trim the beans, add them to the skillet and cook until crisp-tender, 3 to 5 minutes. Drop the beans into ice water for a moment to cool quickly. Drain.

3. Cut the potatoes into quarters and the beans in half. Combine in a large bowl and gently mix in the onions and dill.
4. Combine the salad dressing ingredients in the order given. Coat the salad with half the dressing. Cover everything and refrigerate.
5. Combine the ingredients for the barbecue sauce (include the pineapple syrup). Stir well and set aside.
6. Place the ribs in a Dutch oven and cover with 2 to 3 inches of water. Bring to a boil, reduce the heat, cover and *simmer* for about 30 minutes. Drain and pat dry.
7. Place ribs in a single layer in a large baking dish. Add enough sauce to cover. When cool, cover tightly with foil and refrigerate. Refrigerate the remainder of the sauce.

Suggested Menu

Apple Mint Soup

Barbecued-Indoors Country Ribs with Potato-Bean Salad

Strawberry Islands

At least an hour before your guests are expected:

1. Remove the ribs, reserved sauce, salad and remaining dressing from the refrigerator.
2. Preheat the broiler.

Forty-five minutes before:

1. Place the ribs in the broiler about 4 inches from the source of heat. Broil 3 minutes, turn over and broil 3 minutes longer. Repeat twice (3 times in all) brushing on more sauce as needed. Turn oven off.
2. Check the salad for seasonings.

Just before serving:

1. Place a helping of ribs and sauce on each plate.
2. Add a portion of potato-bean salad.

Ham Loaf
with Spinach-Pear Purée

Serves 6

No ordinary meat loaf, this one is company class. Ignore at your peril

YOU WILL NEED

For the spinach-pear purée:

4 10-ounce packages frozen spinach

1 15-ounce can pear halves

7 tablespoons unsalted butter

For the basting sauce:

1 cup light brown sugar

½ cup water

½ cup cider vinegar

¼ teaspoon black pepper

Pinch of freshly grated nutmeg

For the ham loaf:

6 slices of bread

1 pound lean bulk sausage, at room temperature

1 pound tenderized ham, ground

2 eggs

1 cup sour cream

1 small onion, chopped

2 tablespoons fresh lemon juice

1 teaspoon each curry powder, ground ginger, dry mustard

1/8 tablespoon grated nutmeg

1/8 teaspoon paprika

THE COUNTDOWN

Two days ahead:

1. Take spinach from freezer. When thawed, squeeze as much water out as possible.
2. Drain the pears, discarding the syrup.

3. In a food processor, purée the pears with the spinach. Cover and refrigerate.
4. Make the basting sauce: Combine the ingredients in a saucepan and bring to a boil. Cool, cover, and refrigerate.
5. Cut the crusts off the bread. Coarsely chop in a food processor to make about 2 cups of soft crumbs. Seal in a plastic bag and set aside.

Suggested Menu

Carrot & Orange Soup

Ham Loaf with Spinach-Pear Purée

Flawless Flourless Chocolate Cake

One day ahead:

1. Preheat the oven to 350°. Remove the sausage from the refrigerator and bring to room temperature.
2. After removing all the fat, grind the ham in a food processor.
3. Thoroughly mix the bread crumbs with the ham and the sausage meat.
4. In a small bowl, beat the eggs. Add the sour cream, onion, lemon juice and spices. Mix well.
5. Combine the egg mixture and the meat mixture, form into a loaf and place in a large, oiled, glass baking dish. Bake 45 minutes, uncovered.
6. Take the ham loaf from the oven and pour off the excess fat.
7. Bring the basting sauce to a boil and pour half of it over the loaf. Cool the loaf, cover tightly and refrigerate.
8. Cool the remaining sauce, cover and refrigerate.

... and this is no ordinary host

At least an hour before your guests are expected:

1. Take the ham loaf, spinach purée and basting sauce from the refrigerator.
2. Preheat the oven to 350°.

Thirty minutes before:

1. Reheat the remaining basting sauce, pour over the ham loaf and place the dish in the oven, uncovered.
2. Melt the butter in a large skillet. When the butter begins to foam, pour the spinach-pear purée into the skillet. Add salt to taste and stir until hot. Cover and turn off the heat.

Just before your guests are expected:

1. Check the meat loaf. If sufficiently hot, turn off the oven.

Just before serving:

1. Heat the purée until piping hot.
2. Place a portion of the ham loaf on each plate, spoon a bit of the sauce on top and surround with spinach-pear purée.

Chicken Entrées

What is sauce for the goose
may be sauce for the gander
but it is not necessarily sauce
for the chicken, the duck, the turkey,
or the Guinea Hen.

– Alice B. Toklas

Casablanca Chicken

Serves 6

This gets better and better As Time Goes By

YOU WILL NEED

1 3½-pound chicken, cut up

2 whole chicken breasts, split

5 cups chicken broth

For the vegetables:

¼ cup vegetable oil

2 tablespoons butter

1 large onion, coarsely chopped

4 garlic cloves, minced

5 plum tomatoes, coarsely chopped

1 cup chopped parsley

2 teaspoons each ground ginger, turmeric, and cumin

1 whole jalapeño pepper

2 cinnamon sticks

¼ teaspoon cayenne pepper

1/8 teaspoon crushed saffron threads

5 small turnips, peeled and quartered

3 large carrots, quartered lengthwise and then crosswise

3 zucchini, quartered lengthwise and then crosswise

1 15-ounce can of black-eyed peas, drained and rinsed

1 cup pitted prunes, halved

1 cup golden raisins

Salt and freshly ground pepper

2 10-ounce boxes of couscous

Hot sauce (optional)

THE COUNTDOWN

Two days ahead:

1. Simmer the chicken in the broth in a large Dutch oven until cooked through, about 20 minutes.

2. Remove the chicken from the broth, take the meat off the bones and cut into bite-size pieces. Refrigerate broth and chicken in separate containers.

One day ahead:

1. In a large Dutch oven, heat the oil and 2 tablespoons of the butter over medium heat. Add the onion and garlic and sauté until tender, about 8 minutes.
2. Skim the fat off the reserved chicken broth and add 4 cups of broth to the pot.
3. Stir in the tomatoes, parsley, ginger, turmeric, cumin, jalapeño pepper, cinnamon sticks, cayenne pepper and saffron threads. Boil for 5 minutes.
4. Add the turnips and carrots and simmer for 15 minutes. Cool and refrigerate.

Suggested Menu

Sliced Cucumbers with Orange-Grapefruit Dressing

Casablanca Chicken

No Peel, No Chop, No Cook Delicious Dessert

At least an hour before your guests are expected:

1. Take the chicken and the vegetables out of the refrigerator.
2. Add the zucchini to the Dutch oven and cook the vegetables until crisp-tender, 8 to 15 minutes. Add more broth if needed.
3. Add the chicken, black-eyed peas, prunes and raisins. Remove and discard the jalapeño pepper and the cinnamon sticks. Add salt and pepper to taste and turn off the heat.
4. Cook couscous according to the directions on the box. Fluff and keep warm.

Just before serving:

1. Heat the chicken and vegetables to piping hot.
2. Place a portion of couscous on each dinner plate. Spoon portions of chicken and vegetables on the couscous.
3. Place a small bowl of hot sauce on the table if you wish.

Chicken Breasts & Artichoke Purée with Romaine Couscous

Serves 6

Would that all relationships were so mutually enhancing

YOU WILL NEED

For the chicken:

½ cup flour

Salt and pepper

6 chicken breast halves, boneless and skinless

1 tablespoon butter

1 tablespoon olive oil

For the tomatoes and peppers

1 15-ounce can peeled tomatoes, drained

2 fresh tomatoes, peeled

1 jar roasted red peppers

¼ teaspoon cayenne pepper

For the artichoke purée:

1 14-ounce can artichokes

3 cloves garlic

1 tablespoon olive oil

3 tablespoons chopped fresh rosemary, or 1 tablespoon dried

Juice of half a lemon

For the vinaigrette:

¼ cup olive oil

1/3 cup fresh lemon juice

1 garlic clove, minced

½ teaspoon salt

1 tablespoon water

For the couscous:

1 head romaine lettuce

1/3 cup each scallions, parsley, dill and mint

1½ boxes seasoned couscous (you will need 15 ounces)

THE COUNTDOWN

One day ahead:

1. Mix the flour, salt and pepper in a plastic bag. Add the chicken breasts and shake well to coat.

2. Heat the butter and oil in a skillet over moderately high heat. Add the chicken breasts and cook 5 minutes on a side. When golden brown, remove and place on a paper towel.
3. Place the canned tomatoes and the fresh tomatoes in the skillet, mashing them with a spoon. Add the roasted peppers and cayenne. Heat, stirring, for about 2 minutes.
4. Cool, add the chicken, cover and refrigerate.
5. Drain the artichokes and put them in a food processor. Add the garlic, olive oil, rosemary and lemon juice. Process until smooth. Cool and refrigerate.
6. Combine the vinaigrette ingredients and refrigerate in a covered jar.
7. Wash and dry the romaine. Cut into bite-sized pieces and refrigerate in a plastic bag.
8. Chop the scallions, parsley, dill and mint. Refrigerate.

Suggested Menu

Squash Bisque

Chicken Breasts & Artichoke Purée with Romaine Couscous

Macaroon Pie

An hour before your guests are expected:

1. Take the chicken, artichoke purée and vinaigrette from the refrigerator.
2. Cook the couscous according to the directions on the box. Fluff.

Thirty minutes before:

1. Place the chicken and tomato sauce in a large skillet and heat slowly. Cover and turn off the heat.
2. Add the romaine, scallions, parsley, dill and mint to the couscous. Shake the vinaigrette and stir into the couscous mixture.

Just before serving:

1. Turn the heat high under the chicken for 30 to 60 seconds, stirring.
2. Spoon a portion of the tomato sauce onto each plate. Place a chicken breast on top and cover generously with artichoke purée. Surround with couscous.

Glazed Cornish Hens
with Rice Verde

Serves 6

Like the rest of us, these are remarkable immigrants

YOU WILL NEED

For the hens:

3 large Cornish hens, split in half

Juice of 3 lemons

1 cup Worcestershire sauce

Salt and pepper to taste

1 cup fresh orange juice

¾ cup honey

3 slices of bacon, cut in half

For the rice verde:

Rice to make 2 cups when cooked

1 15-ounce can whole tomatoes

2 10-ounce packages frozen spinach

1 tablespoon fresh lemon juice

3 tablespoons butter

1 large onion, finely chopped

1 teaspoon each ground cardamom, coriander, turmeric and cumin

1 cup tightly packed fresh parsley, finely chopped

THE COUNTDOWN

One or two days ahead:

1. Cook the rice. Cool and refrigerate.
2. Drain and mash the tomatoes. Refrigerate.
3. Defrost the spinach, drain and squeeze dry. Sprinkle with lemon juice. Refrigerate.

To market, to market …

One day ahead:

1. Wash the split hens and pat dry.
2. In a zippered plastic bag, combine the lemon juice, Worcestershire sauce and salt. Add the hens, close the bag and refrigerate.
3. In a large skillet melt the butter and sauté the onion until soft. Lower the heat and stir in the spices. Add the tomatoes, spinach and rice, stirring after each addition. Cool, cover and refrigerate.
4. Wash, dry and chop the parsley, place in a plastic bag and refrigerate.

Suggested Menu

Eggplant Rollups with Herbed Cheese

Glazed Cornish Hens with Rice Verde

Pristine Pears

At least an hour before your guests are expected:

1. Take the rice verde and the parsley from the refrigerator.
2. Take out the hens. Discard the marinade and place the hens in a baking dish. Mix the orange juice and honey and pour over the hens. Lay half a strip of bacon over each one.
3. Preheat the oven to 350°.

An hour before:

1. Place the hens in the oven and bake for 45 to 55 minutes. Turn the oven off and cover.

Fifteen minutes before:

1. Gently heat the rice mixture and cover.

Just before serving:

1. Heat the rice mixture to piping hot.
2. Place half a hen and a portion of rice on each plate. Sprinkle parsley over all.

Ginger Cream Chicken
with Bulghur Pilaf

Serves 6

This is a very polished dish … the crunchy pilaf is a fine foil for the velvety sauce.

YOU WILL NEED

For the pilaf:

1½ cups water

1½ cups bulghur

1 tablespoon olive oil

1 onion

1 teaspoon curry powder

1 red bell pepper

1 large carrot

2 celery stalks

Salt and pepper to taste

½ cup chicken broth (needed when reheating the bulghur)

Where was I?

For the chicken:

6 large chicken breast halves, skinless and boneless

1 teaspoon ground ginger

½ cup flour

Salt and freshly ground pepper

2 tablespoons vegetable oil

4 scallions, minced

For the sauce:

4 tablespoons butter

4 tablespoons flour

2 teaspoons ground ginger

1 cup chicken broth

1 cup Madeira

1 cup heavy cream

8 tablespoons crystallized ginger

Parsley sprigs, for garnish

THE COUNTDOWN

Two days ahead:

1. Boil the water and pour over the bulghur. Cover for 30 minutes.
2. Finely chop the onions, red pepper, carrots and celery.
3. Sauté the onions in the olive oil until soft. Stir in the curry. Stir in the red pepper, carrots and celery.
4. When the bulghur is done, uncover and fluff thoroughly with a fork. Add the vegetable mixture and salt and pepper to taste. Cover, cool and refrigerate.

Suggested Menu

Artichoke Hearts with Roasted Pepper Sauce

Ginger Cream Chicken with Bulghur Pilaf

Oranges Araby

One day ahead:

1. Flatten the chicken breasts to an even thickness.
2. In a paper bag mix the ginger, flour, salt and pepper. Add the chicken and shake until well covered. Tap off any excess.
3. Heat the vegetable oil in a large skillet. Sauté the chicken breasts until golden, three or four minutes on each side, adding the scallions when the chicken is turned. Remove to a plate and set aside.
4. Finely chop the crystallized ginger.
5. Make the sauce: In a medium saucepan melt the butter, add the flour and the ground ginger, and stir well. Gradually add the chicken broth, the Madeira and the cream. Stir until thickened. Add 4 tablespoons of the crystallized ginger. Turn heat off.
6. Butter a large shallow baking dish, place the chicken breasts in the dish without overlapping, and pour the sauce over all. Cool, cover tightly with plastic wrap, and refrigerate.

At least an hour before your guests are expected:

1. Remove the chicken and the bulghur dishes from the refrigerator. Replace the plastic wrap on the chicken dish with foil.

2. Place the bulghur mixture in a medium saucepan. If it seems dry, add a little chicken broth.

3. Preheat the oven to 275°.

Forty minutes before:

1. Place the chicken dish in the oven.

2. After 40 minutes turn the oven off.

Just before serving:

1. Heat the bulghur.

2. Place a portion of bulghur in the center of each plate and lay a chicken breast on it.

3. Cover the chicken generously with sauce and sprinkle with the rest of the crystallized ginger and the parsley.

Fish Entrées

Calvin:	I don't understand this business about death. If we're just going to die, what's the point of living?
Hobbes:	Well, there's seafood . . .

– Bill Watterson

Lemon-Dill Fish
with Sweet Potato Slices

Serves 6

An odd couple, but lovely to look at and delicious to eat

YOU WILL NEED

For the sauce:

¾ cup plain yogurt

4 tablespoons mayonnaise

3 tablespoons lemon juice

3 tablespoons fresh minced dill or 1½ tablespoons dried

¼ teaspoon red pepper flakes

For the poaching liquid:

3 cups white wine

1½ cups water

6 tablespoons white wine vinegar

3 bay leaves

For the sweet potatoes:

5 large sweet potatoes

4 tablespoons olive oil

Curry powder to taste

For the fish:

6 swordfish steaks, or other thick-cut, firm-fleshed fish

Fresh dill for garnish

3 tablespoons capers (optional)

THE COUNTDOWN

Up to three days ahead:

1. Combine the yogurt, mayonnaise, lemon juice, dill and red pepper flakes. Refrigerate.
2. Combine the wine, water, vinegar and bay leaves. Refrigerate.

One day ahead:

1. Peel the potatoes and cut into half-inch slices.
2. Place the potatoes in a bowl, pour the oil over them and toss until coated. Dust with curry and stir gently.
3. Lightly oil a baking sheet.
4. Place the potato slices on the sheet in a single layer, with no overlapping. Cover with foil and refrigerate.

At least an hour before your guests are expected:

1. Preheat the oven to 375°.
2. Remove fish, sauce, poaching liquid and sweet potatoes from the refrigerator.
3. Bake the potatoes, still covered with foil, for 30 minutes. Turn off the oven but leave in the potatoes to keep warm.
4. While the potatoes are baking, pour the poaching liquid into a large skillet, bring to a boil, reduce the heat and add the fish. Cover and simmer over medium low heat until done, 12 to 15 minutes.
5. Turn the heat off and keep tightly covered.

Just before serving:

1. Place a portion of fish in the center of each dinner plate.
2. Spoon sauce over the fish and sprinkle with dill and capers.
3. Surround with sweet potato slices.

Suggested Menu

Leek & Red Pepper Salad

Lemon-Dill Fish with Sweet Potato Slices

Little Ginger Butter Cake with Mango Sorbet

Salmon Fillets
with Leeks, Carrots & Mushrooms

Serves 6

It's hard to believe that such a distinguished dish is so kind to the cook

YOU WILL NEED

3 carrots

4 leeks

¾ pound bean sprouts

¾ pound snow peas

8 ounces shiitake mushrooms

6 salmon fillets, about 5 ounces apiece

For the sauce:

1 tablespoon minced fresh ginger

2 tablespoons minced fresh cilantro

2 cloves garlic, minced

¼ cup soy sauce

1½ teaspoons sesame oil

1¼ cups chicken broth

½ cup white wine

1 bunch scallions, chopped

Salt and freshly ground pepper

THE COUNTDOWN

One day ahead:

1. Peel the carrots and slice them into long, very thin strips.
2. Wash the leeks thoroughly and slice lengthwise into thin strips with just a touch of green showing.
3. Wash and dry the bean sprouts.
4. Wash the snow peas, string and dry.
5. Wipe the mushrooms with a damp towel and thinly slice.

6. Combine the vegetables and distribute evenly in a baking dish large enough to lay the salmon fillets in a single layer.
7. Lay the salmon on top of the vegetables, with the thicker parts of the fillets toward the edge of the dish. Cover the dish tightly with foil and refrigerate.
8. In a mixing bowl, combine the sauce ingredients and stir well. Cover and refrigerate.

At least an hour before your guests are expected:

1. Take the sauce from the refrigerator and uncover.
2. Take the salmon from the refrigerator, uncover and save the foil.

Suggested Menu

Tango Soup

Salmon Fillets with Leeks, Carrots & Mushrooms

Pineapple Victoria with Strawberries

Forty minutes before:

1. Preheat the oven to 425°.
2. Pour the sauce over the salmon and vegetables. Cover *tightly* with the foil and bake for about 20 minutes.
3. Check that the fish is done and turn off the oven.

Will it serve six?

Trout on Wild Rice
with Carrots Vinaigrette

Serves 6

For taste, texture and looks, this can't be beat

YOU WILL NEED

For the rice:

2 cups wild rice, rinsed well and drained

1½ teaspoons salt

6 cups cold water

1 large bunch scallions, chopped

6 tablespoons unsalted butter

For the trout:

6 trout, about ¾ pound apiece, cleaned, boned, heads removed

Salt and fresh ground pepper

3 tablespoons butter

1 lemon, thinly sliced

1 orange, grated

1 orange, thinly sliced

Parsley sprigs for garnish

1 cup fresh orange juice

For the carrots vinaigrette:

1 pound carrots, peeled and grated

½ cup olive oil

¼ cup white wine vinegar

½ red onion, sliced

2 large cloves of garlic, minced

Juice of 1 lemon

Salt and freshly ground pepper

1 cup chopped parsley

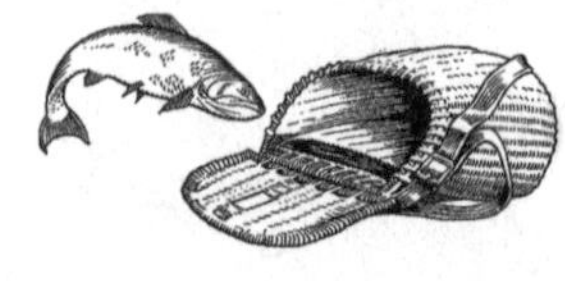

THE COUNTDOWN

One day ahead:

1. In a large saucepan combine the wild rice, salt and water. Bring to a boil, reduce the heat and simmer

until the rice is tender, 35 to 45 minutes. Toss with the scallions and 3 tablespoons of the butter.

2. Butter a baking dish large enough to hold the six trout. Spread the wild rice in the bottom.
3. Rinse the fish in cold water and dry. Salt and pepper the cavities, putting a little butter and a few lemon slices in each.
4. When the rice is cool, arrange the trout on top of the rice. Cover with buttered wax paper and foil. Refrigerate.
5. Grate one orange, slice the other and refrigerate in a plastic bag.
6. Grate the carrots and put in a bowl. In a small saucer, mix the remaining ingredients for the carrots vinaigrette except the parsley. Pour over the carrots and stir with a fork. Cover and refrigerate.
7. Wash, dry and chop the flat-leaf parsley. Refrigerate in a plastic bag.

Suggested Menu

Mushroom Bisque

Trout on Wild Rice with Carrots Vinaigrette

Rum Chocolate Mousse

An hour before your guests are expected:

1. Remove the fish, the bowl of grated carrots and the parsley from the refrigerator. Mix the parsley with the grated carrots.
2. Preheat the oven to 400°.

Thirty minutes before:

1. Carefully pull back the wax paper and foil covering the baking dish. Pour the orange juice over the trout and the rice, and sprinkle with grated orange rind.
2. Cover again tightly and place in the oven for about 30 minutes. Check after 25 minutes. When the trout is flaky, turn off the oven.

Just before serving:

1. Place a portion of wild rice on each plate. On the rice place a trout. On the trout place orange slices and parsley sprigs.
2. Add a serving of the carrots vinaigrette.

Flounder on Ratatouille

Serves 6

Taste and looks belie the ease with which this is made

YOU WILL NEED

For the ratatouille:

3 tablespoons olive oil

2 large red onions , sliced

¾ teaspoon salt

Freshly ground pepper

6 garlic cloves, minced

1 pound eggplant cut into ¾″ cubes

1 long red pepper, cut crosswise into rings and seeded

1 large green pepper, cored, seeded and cut in short strips

1 medium zucchini, cut lengthwise, then into ½″ slices

6 to 8 tomatoes, skinned, seeded and chopped (3 cups)

3 tablespoons chopped fresh basil

½ tablespoon dried thyme or oregano

1/8 teaspoon cayenne

For the fish:

1 lemon, sliced thin for garnish

4 tablespoons fresh lemon juice

4 tablespoons cracker or bread crumbs

6 ounces freshly grated Parmesan cheese

2½ pounds flounder fillets, in six pieces

Salt and freshly ground pepper

Sorry, fellas... but you're going to love the ratatouille

THE COUNTDOWN

One or two days ahead:

1. In a large skillet heat the olive oil. Add the onions, salt and pepper and sauté until soft.
2. Add the garlic, eggplant and peppers and sauté until they are just crisp-tender.
3. Add the zucchini and tomatoes and cook over low heat until *just* tender.
4. Stir in the seasonings. Cool and refrigerate.

One day ahead:

1. Slice the lemon and refrigerate.
2. Squeeze 4 tablespoons of lemon juice and refrigerate.
3. Make the crumbs, cover and set aside.
4. Grate the Parmesan cheese and refrigerate.

At least an hour before your guests are expected:

1. Remove the ratatouille, crumbs, Parmesan and lemon juice from the refrigerator. Butter a large baking dish and scatter half the crumbs on the bottom.
2. Lay the fish on the crumbs in a single layer.
3. Scatter the rest of the crumbs over the fish and drizzle the lemon juice over all. Season with salt and pepper.
4. Spoon the ratatouille generously over all and sprinkle the Parmesan cheese on top.
5. Preheat the oven to 400°.

Thirty minutes before:

1. Place the dish in the oven to bake for 25 minutes.
2. Remove from the oven, cover and keep warm.

Suggested Menu

Prosciutto & Cashew Nut Salad

Flounder on Ratatouille

Peaches Cointreau

Just before serving:

1. With a spatula, lift a portion of fish and vegetables onto each dinner plate.
2. Garnish with lemon slices.

Vegetable & Cheese Entrées

Eating an artichoke is like getting to know someone really well.

– *Willi Hastings*

Eggplant Lasagna

Serves 6

Can you believe it … not a noodle in sight

YOU WILL NEED

For the tomato sauce:

- 1 tablespoon olive oil
- 1 large onion, chopped
- 1 28-ounce can plum tomatoes
- 1 teaspoon each dried thyme and oregano

For the lasagna:

- 2 large eggplants
- 2 medium green or red peppers
- ½ cup olive oil
- Salt and freshly ground pepper
- 6 large eggs, whites only
- 1 pound ricotta cheese
- 1¼ cup freshly grated Parmesan cheese
- ¼ cup chopped fresh basil
- ¼ cup chopped fresh parsley
- ¼ teaspoon cayenne pepper
- ½ pound shredded mozzarella
- ⅔ cup pitted black olives, sliced

THE COUNTDOWN

Two days ahead:

1. Make the tomato sauce: Heat 1 tablespoon of olive oil in a pan, add chopped onion and sauté until soft.
2. Mash the tomatoes and put them in the pan with half their liquid. Bring to a boil, reduce the heat and simmer for 3 minutes.
3. Stir in the herbs, cool, cover and refrigerate.

One day ahead:

1. Preheat the oven to 400°. Take the tomato sauce from the refrigerator.

2. Cut the eggplants crosswise into half-inch slices.
3. Cut the peppers in half lengthwise and remove the core and seeds. Slice crosswise into ¼-inch half circles. Set aside.
4. Line two cookie sheets with foil and brush each sheet with olive oil. Arrange a single layer of eggplant slices on each of the two cookie sheets. Brush the tops of the eggplant slices with olive oil and season lightly with salt and pepper. Bake until tender, about 20 minutes. Cool for a minute or two.
5. In a large oiled baking dish, arrange half of the eggplant slices in a single layer. Set the rest aside.
6. Lower the oven temperature to 350°. Toss the peppers in a bowl with ½ tablespoon of olive oil. Spread the pieces on the lined cookie sheets and bake until slightly softened, about 10 minutes.
7. In a bowl, lightly beat the egg whites. Add the ricotta and 1 cup of the Parmesan, the basil, parsley, cayenne and 1 teaspoon of salt.
8. Spread the ricotta mixture evenly over the first layer of eggplant and follow with 1 cup of the tomato sauce. Next comes a layer of the mozzarella, then the peppers and olives, then another cup of tomato sauce and lastly the remaining eggplant slices.
9. Lightly brush the eggplant with 1 tablespoon of water and sprinkle with the rest of the Parmesan cheese. Cover tightly and refrigerate.

Suggested Menu

Shrimp Salad with Olives, Celery & Snow Peas

Eggplant Lasagna

Lemon Chess Pie

At least an hour before your guests are expected:

1. Remove the lasagna from the refrigerator and uncover.
2. Preheat the oven to 350°.

Thirty minutes before:

1. Place the dish in the oven and bake until thoroughly heated, about 25 minutes.
2. Turn oven off. Lasagna will stay warm until time to serve.

Vegetable Medley
with Coconut Curry Sauce

Serves 6

This vegetable entrée can match the best of meat contenders. And no knives to sharpen

YOU WILL NEED

- 3 sweet potatoes
- 1 head of cauliflower
- 1 medium zucchini
- 1 medium yellow squash
- 1 large red bell pepper
- 1 large onion
- 2 tablespoons vegetable oil
- 2 teaspoons peeled and minced fresh ginger root
- 1 jalapeño pepper, seeds and all, finely chopped
- 1 tablespoon curry powder
- 1 can (5.5 ounces) unsweetened coconut milk
- 1 teaspoon salt
- ½ cup water
- 1 10-ounce box frozen baby peas
- ½ cup dark raisins
- 2 15-ounce cans of black-eyed peas, drained and rinsed
- 1 cup sliced almonds
- Rice for 6 servings

THE COUNTDOWN

Two days ahead:

1. Peel and coarsely chop the sweet potatoes (you will need at least 2½ cups).
2. Coarsely chop the cauliflower (you will need at least 2½ cups).
3. Coarsely chop the zucchini, yellow squash, red pepper and onion.
4. Place the vegetables in separate plastic bags and refrigerate.

One day ahead:

1. Remove the vegetables from the refrigerator.
2. In a large pot, sauté the onions in the oil until soft. Add the ginger, jalapeño pepper and curry powder. Stir constantly for 4 to 5 minutes.
3. Add sweet potatoes, cauliflower, coconut milk, salt and ½ cup of water. Bring to a boil, cover, turn the heat low and *simmer* for about 15 minutes.
4. Add the zucchini, yellow squash, red pepper, peas, raisins and black-eyed peas. Stir well. Cool and refrigerate.

Suggested Menu

Pesto Consommé with Walnuts

Vegetable Medley with Coconut Curry Sauce

Biscotti
Ice Cream

At least an hour before your guests are expected:

1. Remove the pot of vegetables from the refrigerator.
2. Toast the almonds until lightly browned. Set aside.

An hour before:

1. Cook the rice and keep it warm.
2. Put the pot back on the stove and cook over moderate heat until the vegetables are crisp-tender, 10 to 15 minutes. Do not boil. Do not permit vegetables to become mushy. *Check frequently.*
3. Turn the heat off and cover.

Just before serving:

1. Heat to piping hot. Spoon a portion of vegetables onto each dinner plate and surround with rice.
2. Sprinkle almonds over all.

Where did I put the almonds …

Cheese Strata
with Baked Spinach Tomatoes

Serves 6

Good food is good food is good food—and this is good food

YOU WILL NEED

For the strata:

6 slices soft white bread, crusts removed and cubed

5 eggs

1½ teaspoons dry mustard

1/8 teaspoon Tabasco sauce

1½ teaspoons salt

1/8 teaspoon black pepper

Pinch of cayenne pepper

¼ medium onion, grated

2 cups milk

2½ cups extra-sharp Cheddar cheese

For the tomatoes:

6 firm ripe tomatoes

2 pounds fresh spinach

3 tablespoons butter

3 shallots

Salt and freshly ground pepper

THE COUNTDOWN

Two days ahead:

1. Butter a 2-quart casserole. Place the bread cubes on the bottom.
2. Beat the eggs and whisk in the mustard, Tabasco, salt , black pepper, cayenne, and grated onion.
3. Pour the milk into the egg mixture. Mix well and pour over the bread cubes.
4. Cut the cheese into chunks. Place in a processor, pulse until the cheese is crumbly, and spread over the top. Cover and refrigerate.

One day ahead:

1. Core the tomatoes, cut in half and trim the bottoms.
2. In a shallow baking dish arrange the tomatoes, cut side up. Dot with butter and season with salt and pepper.
3. Thoroughly wash the spinach. Put in a large pot and pour boiling water over it. Drain, pressing out as much liquid as possible. Roughly chop.
4. Peel and chop the shallots. Sauté in the remaining butter, stir in the spinach, season with salt and pepper.
5. Place a portion of spinach on top of each tomato half. Cool, cover and refrigerate.

Suggested Menu

Scallops on a Bed of Celery

Cheese Strata with Baked Spinach Tomatoes

Fruit Fondue

At least an hour before your guests are expected:

1. Remove the strata and the tomatoes from the refrigerator.
2. Preheat the oven to 350°.

Thirty minutes before:

1. Place the tomatoes in the oven and bake for 20 minutes.
2. Remove from the oven, cover with foil and set aside.

Just before:

1. Put the strata in the oven to bake for 40 to 45 minutes.
2. When done, turn the oven off, put the tomatoes back in the oven with the strata and leave until time to serve.

Spicy Macaroni with Mulled Grapes

Serves 6

A gourmet version of a comfortable old favorite

YOU WILL NEED

For the grapes:

1 pound seedless green grapes, small and firm

1¼ cups white sugar

⅛ cup cider vinegar

2 to 3 tablespoons water

1 teaspoon broken cinnamon stick

½ teaspoon cloves

1 thin lemon slice

Mint or parsley for garnish

For the macaroni:

2 ounces freshly grated Parmesan cheese

1 cup fresh bread crumbs

4 ounces Monterey Jack cheese with jalapeño, grated

4 ounces extra-sharp Cheddar cheese, grated

3 tablespoons unsalted butter

1 cup finely chopped onions

2 garlic cloves, minced

1 teaspoon ground cumin

¾ teaspoon ground coriander

3 tablespoons flour

3 cups whole milk

1 medium can whole tomatoes (discard the juice)

Cayenne, salt and pepper

12 ounces elbow macaroni

THE COUNTDOWN:

Four or more days ahead:

1. Wash the grapes, discarding any that are soft or imperfect, and place in a non-aluminum saucepan. Add the rest of the ingredients for the grapes and stir well with a wooden spoon.
2. Bring to a boil, reduce the heat and simmer until the grapes turn the color of amber, about 60 minutes. Cool, cover and refrigerate.

One day ahead:

1. Preheat the oven to 375°. Butter a large baking dish.
2. In a food processor grate the Parmesan cheese and make the bread crumbs. Combine and refrigerate in a plastic bag.
3. Grate the Monterey Jack and the Cheddar cheese and set aside.
4. In a large skillet, melt the butter. Add the onions, garlic, cumin and coriander. Cook, stirring, until onion is soft. Stir in the flour and cook for three minutes. Add the milk slowly, stirring constantly.
5. Mash the tomatoes, add to the skillet and bring to a boil. Reduce the heat and simmer briefly, adding cayenne, salt and pepper to taste.
6. Bring a large pot of water to a rolling boil, add the macaroni and boil for 9 minutes. Drain the macaroni and add it to the skillet. Stir in the Monterey Jack and Cheddar cheese and pour into the buttered dish. Cool, cover and refrigerate.

An hour before your guests are expected:

1. Take from the refrigerator the grapes, the macaroni and the bread crumb mixture. Thin the macaroni with milk if needed and cover with the bread crumbs.
2. Preheat the oven to 375°.

Suggested Menu

Mushrooms & Roasted Red Peppers

Spicy Macaroni with Mulled Grapes

Strawberry Tart

Thirty minutes before:

1. Bake until bubbling hot, about 25 minutes.
2. Turn off the heat and keep warm.

Just before serving:

1. Place a portion of macaroni on each plate.
2. Spoon grapes on the side.

Desserts

Excess on occasion is exhilarating. It keeps moderation from becoming a habit.

– W. Somerset Maugham

Apples Grand Marnier

Serves 6

If only Eve had tasted this . . .

YOU WILL NEED

¾ cup sugar

Grated rind of 1 orange

¾ cup fresh orange juice

½ cup Grand Marnier liqueur

2 tablespoons butter, cut small

6 large Golden Delicious apples

1 cup heavy cream (optional)

THE COUNTDOWN

One day ahead:

1. Preheat the oven to 350°. Butter a deep baking dish.
2. In a large saucepan, combine the sugar, grated orange rind, orange juice, Grand Marnier and butter. Bring to a boil, stirring until the sugar is dissolved. Set aside.
3. Peel and core the apples and cut into ¼-inch slices. Lay the slices in the baking dish and pour the Grand Marnier sauce over them.
4. Bake uncovered for 40-45 minutes, stirring frequently so that the apples cook evenly.
5. Remove from the oven, cool, cover and refrigerate.

At least an hour before your guests are expected:

1. Take the apples from the refrigerator. Preheat the oven to 375°.

Just before:

1. Place the apples in oven and immediately turn the oven off.

Serve: With heavy cream if you wish.

Biscotti Ice Cream

Serves 6

Smooth and piquant as an evening at La Scala

YOU WILL NEED

12 chocolate-covered, or other, biscotti

1½ quarts coffee ice cream

¼ teaspoon ground cinnamon

⅛ teaspoon ground cloves

THE COUNTDOWN

Two or three days ahead:

1. Place a large glass bowl in the freezer to chill.
2. In a food processor, coarsely chop 6 pieces of biscotti.
3. Take the ice cream from the freezer and allow it to soften in the refrigerator for 5 to 8 minutes.
4. Spoon the ice cream into the chilled bowl. Working quickly, add the chopped biscotti, cinnamon and cloves and mix thoroughly. Lay a sheet of plastic wrap directly on the ice cream. with another sheet of plastic, cover the bowl tightly and return it to the freezer.

Just before serving:

1. Place a portion of ice cream on each dessert plate
2. Place a whole biscotti beside it.

Good to the last lick

Bronzy Bananas & Apricots

Serves 6

Mellow out with this

YOU WILL NEED

½ cup chopped pecans

¼ cup granulated brown sugar

1 16-ounce can of apricot halves, drained

1½ large ripe bananas, cut into rounds

Rind and juice of 1 lemon

¼ cup bourbon whiskey

3 tablespoons butter

1 cup crème fraîche

THE COUNTDOWN

One or two days ahead:

1. Preheat the oven to 375° and butter a 9″ glass pie dish.
2. Sprinkle half the brown sugar and half the nuts in the bottom of the dish. Arrange apricot halves around the outer edge of the dish and bananas in diminishing circles in the center.
3. Grate lemon rind over the fruit and squeeze lemon juice over all.
4. Pour the bourbon over the fruit and sprinkle with the rest of the sugar and the nuts. Dot with remaining butter.
5. Bake in upper half of the oven for approximately 45 minutes. The fruit is done when the top has lightly browned and the liquid has thickened. Cool, cover with foil and refrigerate.

At least an hour before your guests are expected:

1. Remove the bananas and apricots from the refrigerator.

Fifteen minutes before:

1. Preheat the oven to 350°.

Just before:

1. Place the dessert in the oven and immediately turn the oven off.

Just before serving:

1. Remove the dessert from the oven and put a portion on each plate.
2. Top with crème fraîche.

Chocolate Brandy Pudding Cake

Serves 6

A chocolate lover's dream, and the sauce is inside

YOU WILL NEED

1 cup sifted flour
½ teaspoon baking soda
2 teaspoons baking powder
1/8 teaspoon cinnamon
¼ teaspoon salt
1 cup sugar
½ cup cocoa powder
½ cup milk
1 teaspoon vanilla
¼ cup vegetable oil
½ cup packed dark brown sugar
¾ cup very hot water
¼ cup brandy
1½ pints vanilla ice cream

THE **COUNTDOWN**

One or two days ahead:

1. Preheat the oven to 350°. Butter a 9-inch deep-dish pie plate.
2. Combine the flour, baking soda, baking powder, cinnamon, salt, ¾ cup of the sugar and ¼ cup of the cocoa. Add the milk, vanilla and vegetable oil. Mix thoroughly.

3. Scrape the batter (it will be quite thick) into the pie plate. Cover the top, first with the brown sugar, then with the rest of the cocoa, and finally with the remaining granulated sugar. Pour the hot water and the brandy evenly over the top.
4. Bake until the top begins to bubble and the cake pulls away from the sides, 25 to 30 minutes. Cool on a rack, cover and refrigerate.

One hour before your guests are expected:

1. Remove from the refrigerator.

Just before serving:

1. Spoon a portion of pudding cake on each dessert plate and top with a scoop of vanilla ice cream.

Cook's Special Dessert

Serves 6

Good any old time

YOU WILL NEED

1 grocery store, or

1 cheese shop, or

1 gourmet food shop, or

1 fruit stand

THE COUNTDOWN

At least an hour ahead:

1. Go buy it.

Just before serving:

1. Unwrap it or remove it from the box.
2. Destroy the evidence!

Fantastic Fruit Compote

Serves 6

A combination of "Plain Jane" ingredients that is just plain delectable

YOU WILL NEED

1 seedless orange

½ lemon

¾ cup dried apricots

¾ cup pitted prunes

1½ cup white grape juice

1 cup apple juice

¼ teaspoon each ground cloves, ground nutmeg, ground cinnamon

1 Golden Delicious apple, peeled, cored, quartered and thinly sliced crosswise.

THE COUNTDOWN

Two or three days ahead:

1. With the skin on, halve the orange lengthwise, then thinly slice crosswise. Do the same with the half lemon.
2. In a large Dutch oven put all the ingredients, including the seasonings, except the apple.
3. Bring to a boil over medium heat. Reduce the heat, partially cover and simmer for about 30 minutes.
4. Remove from the heat and add the apple slices.
5. Cool, cover and refrigerate.

At least an hour before your guests are expected:

1. Remove the compote from the refrigerator.

Flawless Flourless Chocolate Cake

Serves 6

So delicious and so easy ... dedicated to those who think they can't bake

YOU WILL NEED

For the cake:

1 stick sweet (unsalted) butter

Aluminum foil

1 large orange

1 cup almonds, with skin on

1 slice stale white bread

4 squares semi-sweet chocolate

⅔ cup sugar

3 eggs

For the glaze:

Slivered almonds, for garnish

2 squares unsweetened chocolate

2 squares semi-sweet chocolate

¼ cup butter, cut up

2 teaspoons honey

THE COUNTDOWN

One or two days ahead:

1. Cut the butter into small pieces and bring to room temperature.
2. Preheat the oven to 375°.
3. Line the bottom of an 8-inch round cake pan with a circle of foil. Butter the foil as well as the sides of the pan.
4. Grate the rind of the orange, avoiding the white pith.
5. In a food processor, finely chop the almonds and the bread.
6. Melt the chocolate squares in a glass bowl over a saucepan of simmering water. Cool.

7. In another bowl, beat the butter until very soft and light. Add the sugar gradually, beating constantly.
8. Add one egg at a time, beating vigorously after each addition.
9. Add cooled chocolate, orange rind, almonds and bread crumbs. Mix thoroughly. Pour into the buttered pan and bake for 25 minutes.
10. Remove from oven and cool for 30 minutes on a rack. Turn cake over onto a rack or a plate. Discard foil. Center of cake will appear undercooked. Relax—great taste and texture! Cool.
11. Make the glaze: Toast the slivered almonds until lightly browned. Slowly melt the two chocolates, the butter and the honey in the top of a double boiler.
12. Remove from the heat and beat until cool and beginning to thicken.
13. Pour the glaze over the cake and tip so the glaze spreads evenly over the top and sides. Smooth with a spatula if necessary.
14. Rim the top of the cake with the toasted slivered almonds. Refrigerate.

At least an hour before your guests are expected:

1. Take the cake from the refrigerator. Bring to room temperature before slicing or the glaze will crack.

I knew I shouldn't have invited more than six

Fruit Fondue

Serves 6

A fun dessert—dip and mix with a choice of sauces

YOU WILL NEED

For the fruit:

Fresh fruits that can be cut into bite-sized pieces and hold their looks overnight. Melons, oranges, grapes and strawberries work well.

For the sweet-sour cream sauce:

Juice of 1 large lime

1½ cups sour cream

Sugar to taste

For the chocolate sauce:

¾ cup strong coffee

9 ounces semisweet chocolate

½ cup sugar

For the raspberry sauce

2 10-ounce packages frozen raspberries

4 tablespoons lemon juice

¼ cup water or fruit liqueur

Sugar to taste, if needed

THE COUNTDOWN

One day ahead:

1. Cut a selection of fresh fruit into bite-sized portions. Place in a bowl, cover and refrigerate.
2. Mix the lime juice and sour cream, adding sugar to taste. Place in a small bowl, cover and refrigerate.
3. Into a double boiler, pour the coffee and the chocolate, slowly adding sugar until the sweetness is to your liking. Cool and refrigerate in a small bowl. Cover.
4. Defrost the raspberries and place in a small saucepan. Add the lemon juice and water (or liqueur). Taste for sweetness and add sugar if

needed. Simmer for two minutes. Press through a sieve. Cool, place in a bowl and refrigerate.

An hour before your guests are expected:

1. Remove the fruit and the sauces from the refrigerator.

Just before serving:

1. Place a serving of assorted fruit on each dessert plate. Provide forks for spearing.
2. Place the three bowls of dipping sauces on the table.

Gingered Ice Cream
with Strawberry-Rhubarb Sauce

Serves 6

Abracadabra!

YOU WILL NEED

For the ice cream:

1½ quarts vanilla ice cream

1 cup crystallized ginger, cut fine

For the sauce:

1 pound fresh rhubarb

1½ cups strawberries, fresh or frozen

⅔ cup or more of sugar

Fresh lemon juice to taste

THE COUNTDOWN

Two or three days ahead:

1. Put a bowl in the freezer to chill.
2. Take the ice cream from the freezer and put it in the refrigerator until just soft enough to stir, 5 or 6 minutes.

3. Take the chilled bowl from the freezer. Spoon the ice cream into it.
4. Working quickly, mix the ginger thoroughly into the ice cream. Lay one sheet of plastic wrap on the surface of the ice cream. with a second, tightly cover the top of the bowl. Return to the freezer.

One day ahead:

1. Chop the rhubarb. Defrost or slice the strawberries.
2. Put the rhubarb, strawberries and sugar into a large, non-stick skillet. Cover and cook over low heat until the juices of the fruit are released, about 5 minutes. Uncover and cook the fruit until tender.
3. Add water if needed. Add lemon juice and more sugar if desired.
4. Cool, cover and refrigerate.

Just before serving:

1. Spoon a portion of ice cream onto each dessert plate.
2. Spoon rhubarb sauce over the ice cream.

Lemon Chess Pie

Serves 6

This pie, a great gift from the South, just never goes out of style

YOU WILL NEED

1 ready-made crust for a 9″ pie

4 eggs

$1^1/_3$ cups sugar

4 tablespoons buttermilk

2 tablespoons cornmeal

Pinch of salt

¼ cup melted butter

Grated rind of 1 lemon

¼ cup lemon juice

You are on your way to making lemon juice

THE COUNTDOWN

One day head:

1. Partially bake the pie shell, according to its directions.
2. When done, remove the shell from the oven and reset the oven to 400°.
3. In a medium bowl, beat the eggs lightly with a fork. Beat in the sugar with a fork or a whisk. Stir in the buttermilk, cornmeal and salt.
4. In a steady stream, pour in the melted butter and stir until smooth.
5. Stir in the grated lemon rind and juice until just incorporated. Pour into the pie shell.
6. Bake for 10 minutes. Reduce the heat to 325° and bake until the filling is set, about 30 minutes. Cool, cover and refrigerate.

At least an hour before your guests are expected:

1. Take the pie from the refrigerator and uncover.

Little Ginger Butter Cake with Mango Sorbet

Serves 6

Butter? You'll miss it when the cows leave home

YOU WILL NEED

- 2 sticks soft butter
- 1 cup sugar
- 1 egg
- 2 cups of sifted flour
- 6 tablespoons finely chopped crystallized ginger
- ½ teaspoon salt
- 1½ pint mango sorbet

THE COUNTDOWN

One day ahead:

1. Preheat the oven to 350°. Cream together the butter and the sugar.
2. Beat the egg. Set aside 2 teaspoons.
3. Add the flour and the rest of the beaten egg, alternately, to the sugar and butter mixture. Add the ginger and the salt. Mix well.
4. Press into an 8-inch pie plate. Brush the top with the reserved egg.
5. Bake for 30 minutes, cool and cut into 6 wedges. Cover tightly.

Just before serving:

1. Place a wedge of ginger cake on each plate with a scoop of mango sorbet beside it.

Macaroon Pie

Serves 6

This little Cinderella pie turns into a dessert fit for a Prince

YOU WILL NEED

¾ cup finely chopped walnuts

24 2″-square graham crackers

¾ cup sweetened flaked coconut

6 egg whites

¼ teaspoon salt

1½ teaspoons almond extract

1¼ cups sugar

2/3 cup heavy cream

2/3 cup *light* sour cream

3 teaspoons confectioners sugar

THE COUNTDOWN

One or two days ahead:

1. Preheat the oven to 350°. Generously butter a 9-inch pie plate.

2. In a food processor crumb the graham crackers. Add the walnuts and chop fine. Add the coconut and stir. Set aside.
3. In a large bowl, beat the egg whites with the salt and almond extract until they form soft peaks. Add the sugar gradually and continue to beat until the whites form stiff peaks.
4. Fold the crumb mixture into the egg whites.
5. Scrape evenly into the pie plate and bake for 30 to 35 minutes.
6. Remove from the oven and cool on a rack. Cover tightly and refrigerate.
7. In a bowl whip the heavy cream into stiff peaks, gradually adding the sugar. Fold in the sour cream until well mixed. Cover and refrigerate.

One hour before your guests are expected:

1. Take the pie from the refrigerator.

Just before serving:

1. Place a slice on each plate with a scoop of whipped cream on top.

Doing it ahead

Mocha Crème Brulée

Serves 6

Good to the last calorie

YOU WILL NEED

1 large egg plus 6 extra yolks

⅔ cup granulated sugar

1¾ cups heavy cream

1¾ cups milk

2 tablespoons Kahlùa liqueur

1½ tablespoons instant espresso

½ cup light brown sugar

THE COUNTDOWN

One or two days before:

1. Preheat the oven to 325°.
2. In a bowl, whisk the whole egg and the extra yolks. Whisk in the sugar.
3. In a heavy saucepan, over moderately high heat, heat the cream and the milk until the mixture comes just to a boil. Add the Kahlùa and the instant espresso, stirring until the espresso is dissolved.
4. Pour the hot milk mixture into the egg mixture in a stream, whisking. Skim off any froth.
5. Divide custard among six small flameproof custard cups or ramekins. Set them in a roasting pan and add enough hot water to reach halfway up the cups. Bake in the middle of the oven until custards are just set but still tremble slightly, about 40 minutes.
6. Remove the cups from the pan, cool, cover loosely with plastic wrap and chill.

At least an hour before your guests are expected:

1. Set the oven rack so that the top of the custard cups will be 2 or 3 inches from the broiler. Preheat the broiler.
2. Remove the custard cups from the refrigerator and let stand for 30 minutes.
3. Sprinkle brown sugar generously over the custards.
4. Place the cups on a baking sheet in the oven, with the door open. Watch closely. When sugar is melted and caramelized, about 2 minutes, remove at once and set aside until time to serve.

No Peel, No Chop, No Cook Delicious Dessert

Serves 6

A great choice for a hectic week—and such gorgeous colors

YOU WILL NEED

- 1 16-ounce package frozen raspberries, unsweetened
- 1 10-ounce package of frozen strawberries, sweetened
- 1 16-ounce package frozen blueberries, unsweetened
- ½ cup of frozen apple juice concentrate
- ¼ cup water
- 1 tablespoon cornstarch
- Sugar to taste

THE COUNTDOWN

One day ahead:

1. Defrost the frozen fruits in a bowl.
2. In a small saucepan, simmer the apple juice and water for about 5 minutes.
3. Mix the cornstarch with 2 tablespoons of water and add to the saucepan. Heat until the cornstarch is dissolved. Cool.
4. When cool, pour over the fruit and stir, adding sugar if necessary. Cover and refrigerate.

One hour before your guests are expected:

1. Remove from the refrigerator.

Oranges Araby

Serves 6

Chic enough for any sheik . . .

YOU WILL NEED

8 navel oranges

¼ cup honey

¼ cup fresh orange juice

1 tablespoon water

1 teaspoon cinnamon

6 small sprigs of mint leaves

THE COUNTDOWN

Two days ahead:

1. Peel the oranges and cut into ¼-inch slices.
2. In a small saucepan, heat the honey, orange juice and water until the honey dissolves. Cool.
3. Pour mixture over the oranges, cover and refrigerate. Baste occasionally.

When ready to serve:

1. Sprinkle lightly with cinnamon.
2. Top with mint leaves.

Is that the sheik?

Peaches Cointreau

Serves 6

Accept the kudos with grace even though this is embarrassingly simple to make

YOU WILL NEED

- 2 16-ounce cans peach halves
- ¾ cup sugar
- 6 tablespoons butter, at room temperature
- ¾ cup Cointreau
- 3 tablespoons fresh lemon juice
- 1 cup sliced almonds
- 1 cup heavy cream (optional)

THE COUNTDOWN

One day ahead:

1. Preheat the oven to 350°.
2. Thoroughly drain the peaches in a colander, discarding the syrup. Butter a baking dish and place the drained peaches in it, cut side up, in a single layer.
3. In a small bowl beat the sugar and butter together until creamy. Place a generous teaspoonful of this mixture in the center of each peach.
4. Mix the Cointreau and lemon juice together and pour over all.
5. Bake for 25 to 30 minutes, basting at least once.
6. Remove from the oven, cool, cover tightly and refrigerate.

An hour before your guests are expected:

1. Remove the peaches from the refrigerator.
2. Toast the almonds and set aside.

Just before serving the main course:

1. Scatter the toasted almonds over the peaches.
2. Put in a warm oven until time to serve.

Serve: With heavy cream if you wish.

Pears in Red Wine

Serves 6

Timeless ... a favorite of countless dinner guests

YOU WILL NEED

- 6 pears, Bartlett, Bosc or Anjou
- 1 cup light brown sugar
- ¼ teaspoon cinnamon
- ½ teaspoon grated lemon rind
- 1½ cups or more red wine
- 1 cup crème fraîche

THE COUNTDOWN

One day ahead:

1. Preheat the oven to 275°.
2. Peel the pears, leaving the stems intact. Take a thin slice off the bottom of each pear so the pear will stand upright.
3. In a saucepan large enough for the pears to fit snugly, combine the wine, sugar, cinnamon and lemon rind. Bring to a boil, reduce the heat and simmer for 5 minutes.
4. Stand the pears upright in the wine and poach at the lowest possible simmer, basting evenly and frequently so the pears turn a beautiful rich red.
5. When the pears are tender (it may take an hour with considerable basting) turn the heat off, cool, cover, and refrigerate in the sauce.

At least an hour before your guests are expected:

1. Remove from the refrigerator.

Just before serving:

1. Stand a pear on each dessert plate, spoon a bit of sauce over each and add a dollop of crème fraîche.

Pineapple Victoria
with Strawberries

Serves 6

Albert loved it, and so will you

YOU WILL NEED

2 packages fresh pineapple

¾ cup sugar

⅓ cup water

¼ cup Triple Sec liqueur

Zest of 1 orange

¼ cup fresh lime juice

1 cup fresh strawberries

Fresh mint for garnish

It's a pity the queen couldn't make it

THE COUNTDOWN

One day ahead:

1. Cut the pineapple into chunks and place in a bowl. Save the juice.
2. In a small saucepan, boil the sugar and water until the sugar is dissolved. Add the liqueur, orange zest, lime juice and the juice from the pineapple.
3. Pour the mixture over the pineapple. Stir, cover and refrigerate.

At least an hour before your guests are expected:

1. Remove the bowl of pineapple from the refrigerator.
2. Hull and slice the strawberries.

Just before serving:

1. Add the strawberries to the pineapple and stir gently.
2. Garnish with fresh mint.

Pristine Pears

Serves 6

This is elegantly simple, like the little black dress

YOU WILL NEED

1 chilled bowl

6 pears

1/3 cup sugar

2 tablespoons fresh lemon juice

½ teaspoon powdered ginger

3 tablespoons crystallized ginger, finely chopped

1 lemon

Fresh mint leaves for garnish (optional)

THE COUNTDOWN

One day ahead:

1. Put a bowl in the freezer to chill.
2. Peel the pears.
3. Stand one pear at a time on a cutting board and slice down on all sides. Discard the core and the stem. Slice the pear pieces into plump chunks.

4. Combine the pears, sugar, lemon juice and powdered ginger in a heavy saucepan large enough not to crowd the pears. Stir over medium heat until the pears begin to soften.
5. Lower the heat and continue to stir until *just* tender, but not mushy.
6. Remove from the heat and add the crystallized ginger. Cool slightly and transfer to the chilled bowl. Lay plastic wrap directly on the pears, cover the bowl tightly with another sheet of plastic wrap, and refrigerate.

At least an hour before your guests are expected:

1. Remove the pears from the refrigerator.
2. Zest the lemon.

Just before serving:

1. Garnish the pears with lemon zest. And with mint if you wish.

Rum Chocolate Mousse

Serves 6

It's full *of calories … don't worry about it*

YOU WILL NEED

4 large eggs
4 tablespoons unsalted butter
7 ounces semisweet chocolate
Pinch of salt
1 teaspoon vanilla extract
1½ tablespoons light rum
2 tablespoons sugar
1 cup heavy cream

THE COUNTDOWN

One day ahead:

1. Remove the eggs and the butter from the refrigerator and bring to room temperature.

2. Place 6 ounces of chocolate in a glass bowl over a saucepan of simmering water. When melted, stir in the butter vigorously, one tablespoon at a time. Add the salt, vanilla and rum and mix thoroughly.
3. Separate the eggs. Stir each egg yolk separately into the chocolate mixture, beating well after each addition. Set aside.
4. In a clean bowl beat the egg whites until soft peaks form and then, gradually and at top speed, add the sugar. Mix half of the egg whites into the chocolate mixture and then carefully fold in the rest.
5. Whip the cream until soft peaks form and gently fold into the chocolate mixture. Spoon into wine glasses or ramekins, cover and refrigerate.
6. Grate one ounce of the chocolate and refrigerate in a plastic bag.

Just before serving:

1. Sprinkle grated chocolate over each dessert.

Savannah Orange Pie

Serves 6

Honey, you ain't tasted nothin' 'til you have a bite of this

YOU WILL NEED

- 1 ready-made crust for a 9″ pie
- 4 eggs
- 1¾ cups sugar
- Grated rind of 1 orange
- Juice of 3 oranges
- 4 tablespoons butter, cut into small pieces
- 1/8 teaspoon salt

Here's to the cook!

THE COUNTDOWN

One day ahead:

1. Partially bake the pie crust according to the instructions on the package. Remove from the oven and cool.
2. Beat the eggs. Add sugar, orange rind, orange juice, butter and salt. Stir well and let stand for 10 minutes.
3. Turn oven to 325°.
4. Pour pie mixture into the partially baked crust.
5. Cover the outer rim of the crust with strips of foil to avoid overbrowning.
6. Bake in the middle rack of oven for 45 to 50 minutes or until golden brown. The pie will jiggle a little but will become firm as it cools.
7. Cool, cover and refrigerate.

At least an hour before your guests are expected:

1. Remove the pie from the refrigerator and uncover.

Strawberry Islands

Serves 6

Tastes as good as it looks—and it looks sensational

YOU WILL NEED

1½ quarts ripe strawberries, cleaned and hulled

1 tablespoon lemon juice

6 tablespoons sugar

1½ tablespoons Kirsch

For the "islands"

2/3 cup heavy cream

2/3 cup *light* sour cream

1 tablespoon confectioners sugar, sifted

THE COUNTDOWN

One day ahead:

1. Set aside 6 of the best berries for garnish.
2. Put the rest of the berries and the lemon juice in a food processor. Pulse on and off until the berries are puréed.
3. Pour into a bowl, add the Kirsch and the 6 tablespoons of sugar and stir until the sugar dissolves.
4. In another bowl, whip the heavy cream into stiff peaks, gradually adding the sugar. Fold in the sour cream until well mixed.
5. Measure out *half* the strawberry purée and fold it gently into the whipped cream mixture.
6. Into each of six dessert bowls, ladle a pool of strawberry purée and float an "island" of whipped cream on top. Cover and refrigerate.

Just before serving:

1. Top each "island" with a strawberry.

Enjoying your guests

Strawberry Tart

Serves 6

Crunchy shortbread topped with cream cheese and strawberries ... enchanting

YOU WILL NEED

1 stick of butter, sliced

1 cup of flour, sifted

¼ cup confectioners sugar, sifted

8 ounces plain cream cheese, cut into quarters

½ cup granulated sugar

12 ripe strawberries

THE COUNTDOWN

One day ahead:

1. Preheat the oven to 350°.
2. Put the butter, flour and confectioners sugar into a food processor. Pulse 3 or 4 times, until crumbly beads form.
3. Transfer this mixture to a 9-inch pie plate, and press it down, using the palm of your hand or the back of a large spoon. It should end up as a flat circle of even thickness (do not press the dough up the sides).
4. Bake on the middle rack of the oven for 15 minutes. Lower the heat to 325° and bake another 15 minutes. Set the crust on a rack until *completely* cool.
5. Put the cream cheese and the granulated sugar in the food processor. Pulse 3 or 4 times, or until mixed. Spread evenly over the cooled crust and refrigerate.

Thirty minutes before your guests are expected:

1. Take the tart from the refrigerator.
2. Hull the strawberries and arrange them on top.

Wine Red Jelly

Serves 6

Your grandmother had it … you *have it …*
wine jelly never loses its allure

YOU WILL NEED

For the jelly:

2½ envelopes plain gelatin

½ cup cold water

3 cups good Cabernet Sauvignon

½ cup Marsala wine

½ cup fresh orange juice

½ cup sugar

Pinch of ground cloves

For the cream:

2/3 cup heavy cream, chilled

2/3 cup *light* sour cream, chilled

3 tablespoons confectioners sugar

THE COUNTDOWN

One day ahead:

1. Sprinkle the gelatin over the cold water and let stand for 10 minutes.
2. Pour the wines and orange juice into a non-reactive saucepan and heat (but do not boil). Stir in the sugar and the cloves. Add the softened gelatin, and stir until dissolved. Cool.
3. Pour into individual wine glasses, cover and refrigerate.
4. In a glass bowl, beat the heavy cream until soft peaks form. Add the sour cream and confectioners sugar and beat until soft peaks form again. Cover and refrigerate.

Just before serving:

1. Remove jelly goblets and the cream from the refrigerator.
2. Top each wine glass with a dollop of whipped cream.

Acknowledgments

We would like to acknowledge our deep indebtedness to all cooks, professional and non-professional, to writers of cookbooks and editors of food magazines, and to family, friends and acquaintances whose insights and generosity have made this book possible.

We are especially grateful to Graydon Upton for his willingness to consume both our failures and successes, to Julia Hill to whom, because of her professional expertise, we listened, and to Nan Starr for her fine work on the cover of this book.

Index of Recipes